Digital Infrastructures of Cognition, Culture, and Democracy

Examining how artificial intelligence and cognitive automation reshape dispositions towards attention, learning and public life, this book offers a critical framework to counter technocratic drift and to rethink agency and democratic responsibility in an increasingly automated world.

Digital Infrastructures of Cognition, Culture, and Democracy rethinks the role of human intelligence and responsibility in environments increasingly guided by automated systems. It develops a critical understanding of how automated decision-making, data-driven platforms and algorithmic infrastructures, alongside neoliberal regimes of evaluation that discipline individual and institutional ethics through measurement, metrics and ranking, are transforming engagement with knowledge and the common good, redefining learning and notions of merit, reshaping social relations and democratic life. With case studies and discussions of emerging digital governance, this book offers new theoretical frameworks and socio-pedagogical strategies for reimagining digital ecosystems and equips readers with conceptual tools to recognise subtle forms of algorithmic power and to cultivate more conscious, reflective uses of digital technologies and the possibilities of algorithmic activism.

This book will appeal to all those in need of analytical tools to assess the societal impact of AI, from researchers and students in sociology, media studies, communication, anthropology, political theory, philosophy of technology and education to professionals working in policymaking, digital governance and public administration.

Vania Baldi is Professor of Sociology and of Cultural and Communication Processes in both Italy and Portugal. His work explores the intersections between media environments, digital infrastructures, political communication, ethics and the social anthropology of technology. With a transdisciplinary approach, he examines how artificial intelligence, platform capitalism and data-driven systems reshape mind, epistemology, public life, education and democratic culture. He has taught and conducted research across multiple institutions and international programmes, contributing to debates on critical media theory, algorithmic governance, epistemological transformations and the socio-political implications of automated decision-making.

Routledge Advances in Artificial Intelligence and Society

This series presents cutting-edge interdisciplinary research examining the complex intersections between artificial intelligence technologies and contemporary society. It explores AI's transformative impact on social structures, cultural practices, ethical frameworks, governance systems, organisational behaviours, and human relationships. It particularly encourages works that critically examine AI's influence on power dynamics, social stratification, and democratic processes, as well as studies investigating public perceptions, policy responses, and regulatory approaches to AI governance.

Titles in this series

Digital Infrastructures of Cognition, Culture, and Democracy
Politics of Disengagement and Artificial Ignorance
Vania Baldi

For more information about this series, please visit: https://www.routledge.com/Routledge-Advances-in-Artificial-Intelligence-and-Society/book-series/

Digital Infrastructures of Cognition, Culture, and Democracy

Politics of Disengagement and Artificial Ignorance

Vania Baldi

Routledge
Taylor & Francis Group
LONDON AND NEW YORK

First published 2026
by Routledge
4 Park Square, Milton Park, Abingdon, Oxon OX14 4RN

and by Routledge
605 Third Avenue, New York, NY 10158

Routledge is an imprint of the Taylor & Francis Group, an informa business

British Library Cataloguing-in-Publication Data
A catalogue record for this book is available from the British Library

ISBN: 978-1-041-28591-5 (hbk)
ISBN: 978-1-041-28592-2 (pbk)
ISBN: 978-1-003-76543-1 (ebk)

DOI: 10.4324/9781003765431

Typeset in Times New Roman
by codeMantra

To Micaela, for her generous, attentive and deeply caring love: a true wellspring of a wonderful life

Contents

Introduction

Digital culture's double bind: minds in the loop amid politicised noise and depoliticised critique

The relationships between our mind, the surrounding environment, the integrated techno-mediatic apparatuses and the ideas that circulate through them and materialise in languages, discourses and orientation of sensibilities make conjecture about the *historical immaterialism* that characterises our time unfounded. Our relationship with the material and inorganic world is constitutive of our cognition which, as described in the first part of the book, we can define as "thinging"; a neologism that means that we do not think *about* things, but always *through* and *with* them.

However, the ecomediatic space is not merely the stage for interconnections between objects, people and info-communication flows, but is the contemporary engine of the political and cultural economy. Its technological devices are not mere instruments, but the matrices of specific conceptions of society and humanity, the moulds of a psycho-anthropological *design*, the levers of particular logics and practices of interaction and valorisation. Therefore, as we shall try to demonstrate in the daily and profound relationships woven with digital services and languages, it is essential not only to observe the adjustments, customisations or anthropological and social adaptations to such services and languages, but also to more deeply verify the transformations in our outlook and assess the nature of social phenomena, our relationship with them and even the way we view ourselves. In other words, to understand whether and how the meaning we project onto our human qualities and social roles has changed.

The computational reconfiguration of the various spheres of social life has not only brought about original and profound transformations in private and public life, but has also reinforced historical and cultural trends that have already been in place in Westernised societies for decades. This has led to structuring the reorganisation (and therefore re-signification) of relations between institutions, markets, governments, the media, educational structures, citizenship exercises, leisure culture, etc. By exploring some of the intersections between socio-technical developments, psychosocial dynamics, ideological axioms and economic interests, this study thus reveals the

DOI: 10.4324/9781003765431-1

contours of a phenomenology of power crossed by diverse tensions between new hierarchies organised in networks and renewed terrains of subjectivation.

In this book, some of the consequences of these tensions are analysed, along with several crucial ethical and cultural challenges that draw our attention to profound epistemological and political changes that are highlighted. The links between neoliberalism and digital technologies have revealed an ideological and operational strategic convergence that paves the way for reducing human relationships to functional interactions. In such interactions, individuals are seen as *interfaces* that store reserves of data, attention, consensus and credit for the *interfaces* of platforms, politics and commerce, each with specific interests mobilised by the logic of *marketing*. In this context, the "qualities" of individuals are always subject to monitoring, and the various *scores* and *rankings* associated with them must be kept up to date.

The instrumental optimisation of cognitive and relational processes, the automatisms of personalisation and economic valuation devices, and the "gamification" of relationships with work and culture have all perverted the communicative dimension into calculative and technicist models. In this regard, personal and professional aspirations have increasingly been shaped by a numerical morality that erodes collective commitment to ambitious shared goals and long-term public purposes. In place of such common horizons, it fosters competitive behaviours oriented toward continuous, measurable gains, in which individuals are compelled to improve their position, consolidate their advantage, and relentlessly pursue ever greater return. It is a pity that such results have no end or purpose, that they represent no moral achievement that transcends the contingency horizon. After all, in the relegation of any ethical or aesthetic vocation, there is a sort of chain of practical tasks to complete, problems to solve and benefits to measure and quantify in a championship where the players are played by the rules of the game they are involved in, and by the anxious excitement of their gamified gains thus obtained.

The disinvestment in comprehensive, long-term common causes is also reflected in the training and education systems, in their design and the definition of their status. Training docile workers who are up to date with market needs appears to represent what psychoanalyst Wilfred Bion would call the "basic assumptions" ("protomental" aspects that induce automatic beliefs and conducts) of meritocratic criteria. Playing with pedagogical methodologies and turning them into training and drills for *problem-solving* in business confirm a utilitarian and standardised view of learning that undoes the emancipatory promises traditionally projected in education. In line with this trend, the sectorisation of specialisms and competences that organise training provision also leads to the institutional production of epistemic ignorance about the interdependencies between the various types of knowledge necessary to understand the intricate dimensions of contemporary reality. Through the studies reported here, we will try to understand whether the dominant rhetoric about "technological solutionism" has also set in chain beliefs and pedagogical practices that converge with the economic and instrumental drift currently associated with education and knowledge. Could it be, in this scenario, that the discourses on meritocracy lead to practices that are conducive to "mediocracy"? (Deneault, 2015).

A backdrop to the book is a critique of the affordances of digital environments, which aim not only to maximise the monetisation of communication within them, but also to standardise interactive practices, making them, as philosopher Robert Pfaller would define them, "interpassive". Such practices have repercussions in the sterilisation of cultural criticism and associative *pathos* and, consequently, in the inhibition of creative and transformative social actions. The paradox is that the *sociopathic sociality* of the WEB seems to vent itself in a furious and general ideologisation of many aspects of daily life. The daily communications and comments that populate news and social media platforms seem to politicise and moralise every pretext provided by social life with hostility and frustration. However, the result of this conflict oscillates between a sense of powerlessness, dispersion and fragmentation of ideas, projects and values that find neither the space nor the time to be shared in a socially constructive manner.

Online sociality is sociopathic because it does not create lasting convergence but is sustained by interactive spaces that stimulate personalism, trends and expectations of constant confirmation, where the interlocutors are interchangeable and the topics too. Interchangeable discourses and interlocutors constitute what Christopher Bollas calls "transmissive selves" (2018). A profound psychological transformation leads individuals to mimic the functions of information-transmission devices, in which the act of conveying information (the transmission itself) often becomes more significant than the substance of what is being shared. Although the language is often imbued with emotional impulses, the participatory attitude that surrounds it is one of prophylactic distance. A form of psychological "dissociation" seems to precede digitally mediated acts of engagement, as if it were an inevitable adaptive mental strategy to permanent connection (Bollas, 2018).

The operational affordances in digital infrastructures and platforms fuel an environment that reinforces processes of individualisation and weakens the socio-political capacity to imagine and organise collective struggle. Those who wish to build bridges, deepen connections, and articulate different points of view outside of trending topics do not find a favourable environment on most digital platforms. In this sense, *politics of disengagement* refer to a less idle and more selective use of digital mediation, as well as a more satisfying pursuit of sociality.

In the context of this socio-cultural and political-economic prism, what we conventionally call Generative Artificial Intelligence also yields an epistemological blockage and projective paralysis in its users. This, being the result of its dependence on predictive systems based on statistical correlations and probabilistic calculations, makes the learning and the decisions to be taken in the present hostage to the past projected into illusorily foreseeable futures. The dimensions of the possible and the incomputable are thus frozen and rejected in the unthinkable, providing knowledge and social experiences that reflect, as in a game of mirrors, inert and conservative expectations.

Throughout this book, "AI" refers not to Artificial Intelligence but to Artificial Ignorance, that is, a system designed to calculate without understanding, to act without thinking, to predict without imagining and to quickly optimise production processes without judging. A powerful technology that effectively fosters habits of dependence, docility, and epistemic inhibition. It denotes a socio-technical regime that outsources discernment, disables critical reflexivity, and converts literacy and consciousness into scripted functionality: a form of programmed unawareness (because ignorant of the data and logic that support computer models and their results) with epistemic and political consequences of deskilling (or "mindless", as Simon Head would say, 2014).

The challenge posed by new large language models (LLMs), however, allows us to think about how to "augment" our intelligence (both social and individual) and how to use these new computational tools for democratically chosen social purposes. Instead of falling into the traps of tech companies' marketing rhetoric and turning these computational tools into oracles designed to please us and reduce our cognitive efforts, we can rise to the challenge of expanding and deepening their cognitive and collaborative opportunities. As argued throughout the book, *critical AI literacy* must contribute to a design of GenAI that does not automate thinking and ignore doubt but rather provokes them.

Cognitive justice is closely linked to democratic justice, which, in turn, depends on the ethical pluralism of information and communication resources. In this sense, the need to redesign digital services and infrastructures from the perspective of public policies is argued, that is, following criteria and metrics that are opposed to those of the financial interests of the big platforms. The reflections and studies contained herein emphasise that *another world* is not ethically or sociologically *possible* without a technopolitical redesign of another Internet.

Another driving force of the reflections presented here is the transformation of our relationship with historical time. Drawing on various theoretical and empirical approaches to the causes and implications (psychological, political, mediatic and socio-technical) of an absolute primacy of "now", we can observe the emergence of a new and paradoxical solidarity, the one that arises from sharing stresses.

If the combination of marketing and digital platforms tends to create the conditions for a society that produces mismatches, the "autarchic" primacy of "presentism" also stands out in the relationships with the different dimensions of temporality that sustain our psyche and our social creativity. Far from representing an epicurean or stoic experience with time itself, it produces a *feverish anhedonia* that we try to escape from by providing or expecting "presents" that last ever longer.

Orphaned by a socially projectable future or one imagined as utopian, we compensate for its absence by investing in practices of anticipating future events defined by some media theorists as regimes of "*pre*-mediation". Thus, we enter into a peculiar *pre*-hermeneutic relationship with events and facts. The constant attempt to anticipate gives the latter a virtual status.

In the society of anticipation fuelled by the opinions market, prediction systems and the monetisation of data-driven interactions, "true" facts correspond to expectations and its prefigurations. In other words, a projection about an event is more effective than its actual realisation, which is relativised by the iteration of new announcements and new anticipations. The expectations of a fact create a greater impression than the fact itself, just as in public relations, communication about an event is considered more valuable than the event itself (unless this doesn't turn out to be a communication event either).

Joseph Vogl (2022) observed that just as occurs in the financial market, where share prices and investments depend on predictions based on information, indications and circulating rumours, likewise in the market of opinions and free expression "we enter a game powered by expectations of expectations where it is a question of observing observations and anticipating possible anticipations" (Vogl, 2022, p. 69). Thus, we go from an idea of truth based on *epistemology* to one rooted in *doxology.* It is no longer a question of looking for relationships between information and facts, or of substantiating the coherence between words, knowledge and things, but rather a question of following the conventions by which the values of information and things are dynamised and estimated "from opinions that reflect opinions about opinions" (Vogl, 2022, p. 70).

Contemporary communication, across professional, institutional and everyday contexts alike, seems to have entered a speculative short-circuit between information, opinions and tautological rhetoric in a competitive vortex that appears to ignore the limits of the real and the rational. Such *unreflective reflexivity* leads us to another challenge: distinguishing what is relevant and meaningful amid "infopinions" that sever their relation to the logical principles of causality and factuality, mutating into a paradoxical crossroads between fable and maths.

Social and political life is thereby undermined by a *rupture in the pact of trust,* feeding doubts about the axioms essential for the affirmation and acceptance of common references. This leads to the ubiquitous experience of mistrust (whether cynical or resigned) that structurally erodes the possibility of a shared collective ethics.

Yet even within a scenario dominated by the digital dispersion of cultural critique, forms of cognitive and affective resistance to expressive and critical flattening continue to persist across the various contexts examined in this book.

References

Bollas, C. (2018). *Meaning and Melancholia: Life in the age of bewilderment*. Routledge.

Deneault, A. (2015). *La médiocratie*. Lux.

Head, S. (2014). *Mindless: Why smarter machines are making dumber humans*. Basic Books.

Vogl, J. (2022). *Capital y resentimiento. Una breve teoría del presente*. Adriana Hidalgo/A. Hace.

1 Between flesh and clouds

Experience and cognition in the technomediatic environment

Introduction

It is hard to think about our various daily habits without considering the technological backdrop that sustains and articulates them. It is hard to imagine such habits without the constant presence of intermittencies woven by digitally mediated interactions, distractions and attentions (Campo & Citton, 2024). Articulation between our various daily habits is structured via a constellation of digital practices which, in turn, constitute the grammar of a new cognitive ecology and a new ontological security. New common habits merge and overlap with the more traditional ones, and, although differentiated, gravitate toward a new condition of socio-technical existence.

Several studies have drawn attention to the consolidation of a digital *habitus* comprising exchanges, sharing, research, raptures, absorptions, worries, euphoria and fears that occur and follow one another (often overlapping) in the meta-context that is the "on-life" world (Floridi, 2015). Behaviours that are mobilised by network technologies tend to simultaneously fragment yet interconnect different daily activities, as well as to oscillate between inert impulsiveness and a sense of sovereign autonomy. Based on an attitude of repeated immediacy, the actions/reactions/interactions magnetically trapped in an irregular chain of communicational requests are mixed with an illusory complacency brought about by a sense of independence regarding the management of one's own connective instruments. Such trends go hand in hand with the automatisms and playful *design* that mould the functionalities of digital services.

For example, over the past few years, various studies on how to seek and analyse information on the web have shown that the average time it takes to decide on the credibility of a website is 2.3 seconds. Typically, this type of *concentration* applies to very diverse types of information: from websites that focus on health or financial promotion, to the buying of trips or training courses. Regardless of what we are looking for, our search practices reveal that in 2.3 seconds, we decide whether or not we want to trust what is reflected on the screen (Robins & Holmes, 2008).

DOI: 10.4324/9781003765431-2

The relationship with the content and the hypermedia format seems to be of a pulsational nature, which has repercussions regarding the way we view and participate in the (fragmented) sphere of public opinion on the web. There is also a tendency to view discussions pre-reflectively, as in the case of sharing *tweets* or voting on Reddit *posts*. In fact, it has been reported that 59% of users in the United States retweet without having read the *tweet* (Gabielkov et al., 2016), and 78% of Reddit users express themselves in favour of or against certain *posts* without having read the content, based solely on the trend determined by the comments of others (Glenski et al., 2018).

Thus, we seem to be facing "circulation for circulation's sake" (Papacharissi, 2014), in a nugatory and cathartic spiral that also affects public debate or intellectual controversies, a flattening of the dialectic reflected by the automated, personalised and seemingly direct way in which we encounter digitally self-centred information, suggestions and services. Self-centred should be understood as not only the personalisation of content or the *design* of *online* social networks, moulded to encourage the construction of identity scripts and narratives, but also as the ideology focused on projecting protagonism onto the user who is idealised as a unique, special individual detached from community ties. This is reflected in the use of the "*i*" in the trademarks that characterise various digital gadgets (iMac, iPod, iPhone, etc.) and numerous Apps (iRelax, iRun, iCommute, etc.), as well as the "you" of "Broadcast Yourself" and the "Me Me Me Generation" label, chosen in 2012 for the cover of *Time Magazine* to represent *Millenials* and which, in fact, is representative of a spirit of the times that spans the various age groups.

To a large extent, the platformatised cultural industries aim to excite in order to involve (promote *engagement*), to turn the user's dispossession of self into a feeling of joyful and energising participation, to disguise *gamified* seduction as an authentic, emancipating and meaning-rich experience (Sadin, 2020). These techniques are even taught in universities, without (the user) realising that they themselves are trapped, and more perversely, in the same bubble of corporate *engagement* (Baldi, 2013, 2020).

Along with culturally induced and shared narcissistic excitement, we are also faced with some of the darker aspects of the "on-life", which become increasingly evident when we analyse in depth the sense of well-being among the various generations with "always on" digital habits. As we will see, symptoms of constant mood disturbance, attention deficit hyperactivity disorder (ADHD) and feelings of ontological insecurity (Markham, 2021) are part of the socio-technical tangle we inhabit. If university students in the United States cannot concentrate on the same task for more than 20 seconds, and skilled workers cannot last longer than three minutes (Savulich et al., 2019), then we have a problem not only of public health but one that is political and directly linked to the ideas of humanity and society being nurtured by the economy and cultural hegemony that governs digital infrastructures and services (Hari, 2022).

Issues such as information clutter, polarisation on social networks, attention dispersed between one notification and another, or addictive tendencies in games and streaming represent a problematic scenario for *homo digitalis* and the *app generation*. This is a scenario promoted by a business model and platform management based on the microphysics of capturing attention, the thesaurisation of reactions, the transfer of protagonism to users and the stream of sensation-stimuli that punctuate notifications, *scrolling* and interactions (always "datafied") between digital companies, commercials, algorithms, screens and users (Andrejevic, 2008; Beer, 2016).

As stated by Adam Greenfield in his *Radical Technologies: The Design of Everyday Life*, contemporary technologies challenge us to "conceive of ourselves as nervous systems in virtual continuity with the world", to recognise the "porosity" of our mediatic experience and to confront our "radical incompleteness" (Greenfield, 2017, p. 33). This is achieved through strategies anchored in promoting a permanent state of alertness in users via countless multiplatform requests aimed at tying them to their pages, thus generating states of "expectation" and "vigilance". Through a set of intermittent gratifications based on *feedback* and periodic updates of the information flow, each of us is subjected to involuntary coaching in "anhedonic" readiness (Fisher, 2009).

Communication without action

At a graduation day talk given to students of the Moholy-Nagy University of Art and Design in Budapest, the philosopher Byung-Chul Han, highlighting the work of Otl Aicher, one of the greatest German graphic *designers* of the 20th century and the leader of the post-war renaissance of German aesthetics, emphasised the regenerating role of "vocation". Vocation, in its various dimensions, fulfils its role by guiding action and thought towards discontinuity in the face of the *already seen* and *already felt* conformism, instilling ethical strength in the search for and the creation of a new look and feel.

Although throughout his speech, Han referred to the German *designer's* great optimism regarding the socially regenerative power of the ethical and aesthetic, artistic and political vocation, in the final part of his speech he concentrated his reflections on the concerns that had affected Aicher in his later years. Directly citing from the *designer's* words:

> We have become incapable of doing anything. We participate in the world through opinion, no longer through interventions, actions and planning. We all see the state of this world, we all know that something has to be done. But we only write appeals. We participate with full awareness in the process whose end is predictable, but there is a danger that we won't be able to do anything about it.[1]

The discarding of maker energy, its effectiveness exhausted during the process of consumption, action reduced in a sterile process of communication, the hypersemiotisation of discourse that replaces the transformative conception of social criticism and depresses the realisation of something new and alternative to the existing one. To participate passively would appear to be a symptom of impotence in the face of what we "see", of the distancing and neutralisation of acting and innovating concretely despite knowing that "something has to be done". From this perspective, exchanging and permuting signs stands out as the post-political and post-historical activity par excellence, where "innovation" does not refer to a transformation of the existing, and the experiences of events are blurred and transfigured by communication processes.[2] As it is in the case of political correctness or *cancel culture*, where it is more comfortable to reduce the general picture of a conflict or a social problem to a question of symbols and language.

Vilém Flusser had already ironically advocated a post-historical shift from "man of action" to "man who plays", from "*faber*" to "*ludens*", from the transformative use of "hands" to the *superficial* use of "fingertips", from "things that can be manipulated" to "ephemeral and eternal non-things" that can only be felt through keyboards, from action to communication. These "non-things", Flusser said, anticipating the techno-aesthetics of *clouds*, "are not present, yet they are at hand": they are "inapprehensible" and "unforgettable" (Flusser, 2010, pp. 100–103).

However, the point here is to understand to what extent the emergence of such critical, creative and constructive powerlessness can be traced back to the radical commodification of cultural processes and the transformation of technological mediation tools and environments. Knowing at the same time, however, how such powerlessness and social dynamics stem from deeper historical transformations that had already been announced in advance in the middle of the last century with the crisis of teleological and progressive conceptions of history and the beginning of the "secularisation" of modernity. Equating the link between the historical, socio-anthropological and techno-political implications of these processes allows us to see the different degrees of disinvestment in the political role of individual and collective life, as well as the loss of ethical and aesthetic efficacy of action.

This is bizarre, given that these critical reflections have a long tradition behind them, for example, in the field of aesthetics, political science or sociology (with roots in the artistic avant-garde or Frankfurt scholars. These reach as far as subaltern and post-colonial studies, or the *post-human* movements, the *cyborg manifesto* and the rescue of vernacular epistemologies). Think of the number of books published every year in the area of multimedia and digital technologies with the title "*for a better world*" (associated with the areas of design and technologies reaches almost 100,000 titles on Amazon). It seems excessive to have such a repeated conviction in wanting to improve the world from a perspective that is so specialised and complicit in the culture of *marketing* and entertainment, so focused on relationships with the means, *layouts*, functionalities or formats of connected technologies. The epistemological concern of these studies most likely does not lie in the ontology of the social world, it does not look at the structures that determine the historical adversities intended to be repaired, nor does it look at the underlying reasons for the malaise spread throughout society, but it does reveal how labels (symbols) overlap with reality. Faced with a social complexity that brings with it challenges and problems that head in the opposite direction to that of "a better world", one would expect a less emphatic belief in the wonders of technology and its languages.

Not all technologists should necessarily be concerned with dealing with the harshness of reality and the urgency of its transformation (not rhetorically, of course, as is the case with speeches focused on technological innovation), nor can it be assumed that they collaborate with social activists, ecologists, public administrators, or that they intervene directly in communities together with NGOs or anthropologists and psychologists. Nevertheless, any technical and aesthetic activity focused on the potential of the expressive form is valuable. What is being emphasised here, however, is the tendency of communication (of "appeals", "opinions", permutations between signs) to replace action: In that sense, "a better world" is more akin to a commercial *slogan*. To envisage a socially promising change based on the experience (of *engagement*) with a technology implies having a vision that is as enchanted and magical about the instruments as it is naive about the realisation of psychosocial transformations, the depth and delay of which inevitably require complex interlocutions, mediations and both affective and social dispositions.

It is as though the logic of *marketing* had crushed the sense of reality, where the playful and performative dimensions infiltrate and replace the critical and creative dimensions, thus conceiving and promoting the *ethos* of the various cultural professions within a horizon of practices mobilised by "gamified" and, at the same time, highly competitive currents: the race to "win points" to gain reputation ("move fast and break things") and the race to resist the impetuosity of programmed obsolescence. An obsolescence that permeates not only the ephemeral life of symbolic and material goods, but also the psychological life of workers in constant competition. A climate that fosters behaviour based on the anxious attempt to anticipate novelties and the related frustration of always having to succumb to the speed of their appearance/disappearance, thus running the risk of falling off the agenda of the discourse that distributes the "points" of recognition (these too being always short-term). Thinking critically can lead to beauty or well-being without having to worry about being *trendy, funny, friendly* or *fancy*.

The symptoms of this socio-communicational drift had already been consistently pointed out by Neil Postman in 1985, in his book *Amusing Ourselves to Death: Public Discourse in the Age of Show Business*. By photographing the trivialisation and decline of American public discourse, he denounced the social consequences of the inroads that *marketing* logic and technique were making in television language and production. Through a reflection on the "epistemology of the media" and the cultural tendency to make sport of the more serious aspects of social life, as in the case of education with the rhetoric of the renewal of didactics through games, or in political life sliding towards a logic of mediatic performativity, Postman highlighted the relevance of Aldous Huxley's prophecy that most people would love technological novelties because by promoting youthfulness and fun, they would be freed from the burden of thinking about and dealing with the causes of social difficulties, and could concentrate only on the promises of novelties.

To go back to the ethical role of communication sciences and technologies, as well as that of design, it is worth mentioning some programme proposals within these disciplines that are trying to change the focus of their objectives in order to respond to the contemporary criticalities occasioned by digital innovations and the disruptive consequences of our development models. What has been proposed to get round these are *undesign* strategies – *undesigning the interaction* (Pierce, 2014) and *undesigning the Internet* (Widdicks et al., 2018). These are studies focused on designing systems that help to *not do* what is acknowledged to be socially harmful. It is a form of scepticism applied to the non- (or inhibited) use of certain technological functionalities whose abuse has proved, or could prove, counterproductive for users, or for the social good of a community. It is a constructive scepticism, critically and reflexively committed to deconstructing the reasons why some technologies are developed in a way that distracts, excites, simplifies, wastes, disempowers, inhibits, de-socialises, creating the conditions for them to be identified as "negative commons" (Bonnet et al., 2021).

This is the cultural manifesto of a group of philosophers and designers who, under the banner of an "ecology of dismantling" (*écologie du démantèlement)*, have aimed their criticism towards the omnipresence of negative common goods. While we spontaneously tend to consider the sharing of common goods as drivers and protectors of positive goods (breathable air, drinking water, education, legality, etc.), these authors point to those infrastructures that are undeniably common (because they currently sustain our existence), yet are inevitably negative (because they threaten our well-being and destinies).

To dismantle, remove the cover, implies to simultaneously rethink another aesthetic and value-system for the future of our infrastructures. We will see below how *design's* contributions play a socially fruitful role when associated with alternative epistemologies committed to dismantling the dominant monocultures within their own area of activity. And when committed, in parallel, to valuing the practical "pluriverse" know-how present in the local communities where they intend to intervene (Andrade & Ibarra, 2021).

All of these questions ask us about the ethical and political dimensions of acting and intervening critically in our time, and what the conditions are for exercising critical thinking in a contemporary world where numbers and neoliberal individualism hold sway. They also ask about the possibilities of these questions at least finding answers through the help provided by the infrastructures of social mediation redesigned by the digital world.

It is well known that the infosphere, by re-ontologising the social world, has created the conditions for the most diverse publishing projects. It has been proven that the web provides the stage for countless groups that follow specific tastes, styles and worldviews, and also that its infinite space hosts political struggles and instances of identity reflected at other local and transnational levels. The heterogeneity of socio-cultural, commercial, artistic and political processes on the web certainly reflects the gigantic number of globally active Internet users. However, while we see there are original experiments in different areas of cultural and civic production, we also see their fragmentation into dispersed and isolated niches, with little penetration into an economy of scale (Poell et al., 2021).

The era of "convergence culture", hailed by Henry Jenkins in 2006 as the new scenario for promising media practices of *online* collaborative creativity, actually refers to the possibility of the new digital media allowing the use of different supports, formats and platforms for the creation and sharing of different contents, but in an unstable production context and with audiences nebulised throughout only partially articulated activities. The migrations of audiences between various platforms, pointed out by Jenkins (2007) as indicative of an unprecedented creative wave, have proved to be the opposite of convergence. Rather, they represent entropic phenomena whose repercussions have been reflected in fluctuating collaborations restricted to fragmented niches, where the ethics and subcultures of *fans* have also been exhausted and reduced to performing the irregular activities of *followers*, i.e. in a typically "liquid" and volatile version of networked cultural practices.

Thus, the question that arises and challenges us is to understand to what extent we can consider digital practices intended to intervene in reality, and that are based on markedly technological and communicational competences, to be civically and socially significant. In order, therefore, to better understand their matrices, their semantics and their legacies, and before focusing on the strictly technomediatic dimensions, it is necessary to quickly recall the historical horizon within which these issues have developed.

The contemporary "regime of historicity", characterised by a relationship with temporality flattened into the "now", is summed up by the term "presentism" to mark the loss of enthusiasm for the future and the commemorative decline that affects the relationship with time that is passing (Hartog, 2003). This reduction of the temporal perspective to the present time, or the present of time, was a timely announcement put forward in the philosophy of technology and philosophical anthropology in the second half of the last century. It was seen as the consequence of a link between the decline of progressive philosophies of history and the emergence of a new techno-instrumental organisational axis of society; an implosion of the philosophical-historical schemes of modernity mirrored by the decisive split between a traditional "hypertrophy of promise" and the "poverty of the existing".

It was with these terms that Reinhart Koselleck (2004), in his book *Future Past. Towards a Semantics of Historical Times*, described the crisis of the worldview of Western modernity. For Koselleck, the ethical and political mission of modernity had been structured around a conception of historical meaning projected onto a unidirectional and linear time vector. In other words, through an indistinct progressive metaphysics, in which a constant tension had arisen between the "horizon of expectation" and the "space of experience". The crisis of the symbolic constellation of *cumulative* and *irreversible* temporality, of Hebrew-Christian origin, leads to the *caesura* of this tension between expectation and experience, reconfiguring an historical semantics within which the current post-historical emotive tone emerges. This is characterised by a sense of emptying of the symbolic charge of the future (the routinisation of its narration) and its reduction to a *dejà vu* or a past future.

The challenges for the ethical and aesthetic ambitions projected in the culture of technological mediation involve deconstructing an "order of time" whose "time-consuming" is mobilised by techno-instrumental reasons and by permanent acceleration. The course of this is largely defined by the fetish of novelty and the constant pitting of everyone against everyone in many areas of social life. We therefore need to understand whether mediatic practices and the technological scenarios that support them also reflect the logic of an autarchic and self-referential presentism, reinforcing an idea of progress that is more symbolic than concrete. By deconstructing this scenario and its psychosocial outspreadings, we can glimpse the cracks through which other types of experiences can be aligned and thus cultivate consistent expectations. To do this, however, it is important to start by looking at the various cognitive mechanisms that underlie these outspreadings and which, in turn, can be activated by them.

Embodied cognition and the body as a prosthesis for digital technology

It is becoming ever more commonplace to portray the infosphere and digital technology as the driving forces behind radical transformations in several spheres: in economic and political life; in the organisation of work and mobility; in our relationships with knowledge and institutions; and also, of course, with the *media* and all those who weave the affections and interests of our daily lives. Less obvious is the way they mobilise peculiar cognitive and emotional, perceptual and speculative processes.

In fact, a more subtle challenge would be to consider the repercussions of the current socio-technical scenario (although, as mentioned, not exclusively determined by it) on the way we live and view temporality, intimacy, well-being, curiosity, individuality, projectivity, social criticism, creativity, involvement with others and self-perception of one's own presence and sense of belonging to the surrounding environment (Campo & Citton, 2024).

To explore these (strictly interconnected) heterogeneous dimensions of subjective and collective experience, viewed from the perspective of the reconfigured technomediatic prism, we will instead turn to theoretical and empirical contributions from the cognitive sciences and the philosophy of technology. These heuristic perspectives make it possible to analyse less visible but more profound aspects of our relationships with our environment and the artefacts that comprise it. Based on this knowledge, we will return to the specific experience of mediation in the context of platformisation and its cultural economy.

Part of our "mind" derives from the material conditions and contexts that objectively make our experiences possible. As explained below, mind is understood as *embodied cognition*, with its processes of incorporation (*embodied*), integration (*embedded*), extension (*extended*) and enaction (enactive) that emerge through interaction with the external world. These are processes that make the mind irreducible to the brain and open it up to particular processes of symbolic and material meaning (Varela, 1997; Thompson, 2007; Newen et al., 2018).

The 20th century left us a legacy of important lessons about the anthropological repercussions associated with the material space we live and grow up in. These teachings remind us that the environment *makes*, constitutes and predisposes the cognitive, affective and sensory faculties of humans. The notion of the environment referred to here is not, therefore, the romantic one of an ecological sphere that is always equal to itself, and that before which we would be spectators. On the contrary, it is one that sees nature and culture as inevitably intertwined, where the environment is considered to be "naturally" cultural and artificial; that is, technologically and linguistically elaborated and reconfigured, but also conceived as a *material agent* that guides the behaviour of the beings that act in it (von Uexküll, 1982; Malafouris, 2013; Latour, 2015).

If we want to understand the relationships we have with culture and contemporary technomediatic products, we have to ground ourselves, first of all, in the heuristic of *material engagement* (Malafouris, 2013), according to which our mind is the product of our being anchored to the inorganic world and to the *material signs* available to us. These, upon acting on our perceptions, reveal an "enactive" role by guiding and transforming the cognitive process into concrete dynamics of operationalisation and sensomotricity. In accordance with this perspective, relations of codetermination and coevolution are established between the practices in which we engage with things and the emergence of our mental and symbolic habits: "we make things which in turn make us" (Ihde & Malafouris, 2019, p. 195).

Material "agentivity", that is, the "enactive" property of signs and artefacts involved in stimulating our reaction and thus triggering a process of reciprocal adaptive negotiation, reveals how much human action depends on the things with which it interweaves its relationships. This is why any hierarchical presumption (or ontological primacy) between individuals and the things that make up their *habitat* is dismantled. In this sense, the individual is just one of the elements that make up the chain of equal relations with the inorganic world.

In the dynamic tension that characterises the process of material engagement, sometimes it is the thing that becomes an extension of the person. At other times, it is the person who becomes an extension of the material agent (Malafouris, 2013, p. 147).

The adaptive interactions taking place within this process of material involvement can lead to ideational (*embedded imagination*) and effective transformations of properties of the material world. As the interactive procedure unfolds, new possibilities for organising the relationship between the organic and inorganic emerge (in a process similar to that defined by Chomsky in his philosophy of language regarding "rule-making creativity") to determine a remodelling of the combinations (cognitions) between organic and inorganic activities (Montani, 2022).

These processes confirm how our relationship with the material and inorganic world is constitutive of our cognition. In light of this, Malafouris (2020) came to define the neologism *thinging* to affirm that we do not think *about* things, but *through* and *with* them.[3]

As has been said, things can extend us prosthetically, on the one hand, and, on the other, it is we who can become the object of the extension. In a digital context, this relationship becomes more complex. Contrary to the position on the age of electricity represented by McLuhan, who in *Understanding Media* conceived of technological means as *externalising/extending* human capacities, in the digital age we are faced with phenomena that also lead towards *internalising* them. Internalisation is understood as the use of some of our bodily organs (as in the case of the retina or the skin, which we will analyse later), which are seen as integrated parts of digital applications that use our organic support to perform their technological functions.

Google Glass, for example, re-launched on the market in 2019 with an *Enterprise Edition 2*, is described as a *heads-up display* that involves *eye tracking* technology and works via *retinal projection*. Our retina would be the screen onto which information is projected from a physical micro-display (*near eye display*) located on the glasses. Without utilising our retina, it would be impossible to benefit from augmented reality through Google's glasses.[4]

Another typical example of technological internalisation involves our largest organ, the skin. There are *smart* temporary patches or tattoos that are used to monitor and show data about our health, acting as a *display*, and others that are used as *trackpads* to manage *displays* or act as touch interfaces for exchanging and sharing data. Our skin would become a *touch-screen*, which, when touched with our fingers, returns information to us, performing the function of *augmented skin*.[5] These and other examples (such as the biometric cryptocurrency "Worldcoin", realised by OpenAI, based on personal identification through iris *scanning*) take us back to a scenario where our corporeality functions as a "quasi-prosthesis" ("quasi" because it is a temporary mediator between organic and inorganic) of connective technology (Carbone, 2020).

In short, "naturally" fitted in among the countless elements that today make up and amplify our environmental reality are the means of communication (from the electricity grid to artificial intelligence systems, the post office, credit cards and satellites), as well as the circulation of their various messages; the sensors that we carry on our bodies, and the IT infrastructures that filter and mediate all these links between objects, brands, information, people and organisations.

In keeping with the above, but with a greater degree of complexity, our approach to the world, whether concrete or abstract, as well as our proprioceptions and tendencies to be more or less self-reflexive, are based not only on the chain of actions and feedback activated by the predefined materiality of the surrounding space, but also by the flow of the mediatic ecosystem in which we are immersed.

Thus, uninterrupted connections, hypermedia languages, and *streaming* communications all participate in the co-creation of our "minds", which results from permanent training with the things and non-things through which we communicate: platforms and *apps*, images and *emojis*, advertisements and algorithms, status updates and notifications, among others, weave the shifting backdrop of our psychic and physical experience with the social network.

Digitally connected devices, therefore, challenge a different polarity in the relationship between bodies and things. Acquiring experiences with and through connective technologies, being involved and becoming involved in a joint process of incorporation and adaptation with them, challenges new enactive forms of symbolisation and action. Given the porosity of our cognition in the face of normal material interference, the new digital devices we currently deal with, designed and programmed to determine specific responses, sensitivities, sharing and attitudes, determine another scenario of cognitive "coupling" (Simondon, 1958).

To what extent, we might ask ourselves, is our ability to adapt to the objectivity of the material world transposable to our relationships with digital environments? To what extent can we plastically reconfigure the rules that internally organise our relationships with automated programmes ("rule-making creativity"), thus projecting meanings onto them that are different from those that are predefined?

Between *habitus* and *affordances*: the interpassive experience

We thus enter an analytical and empirical scenario where at least three agents intervene: physiological causality, technological causality and, challenged by the latter, something similar to what anthropologist Alfred Gell called "a second-order *agentivity* that artefacts acquire within a given structure of social relations" (Gell, 1998, p. 17).

If previously we highlighted the contribution of cognitive sciences with regard to framing the way environmental and material contexts mobilise special mental processes, we can now highlight some contributions from *media* epistemology and cultural anthropology to broaden our understanding of behavioural processes related to mediatic transformations within these same environments. If, through *material engagement*, we considered the retroactive effect that predefined material spaces can have on the cognitive genesis of individuals, the relationships of mutual adjustment with the mediatic environment now encompass entities whose definitions are constantly in flux through the function exercised by the constant intermediation suggested by ever-emerging socio-technical actors (Grusin, 2010).

In this sense, the research field known as *media ecology* has helped define an epistemology based on the impact that technological and mediatic transformations have on various aspects of cultural life and social psychology. According to the perspective developed by the school founded by Neil Postman, these transformations are neither additive nor subtractive. While they neither add anything particular *to*, nor take anything particular away *from* the cultural environment in which they radiate and take root, they generate a general change in the conditions of experience. Therefore, the structure of our anthropological dispositions changes. In other words, the new mediatic environments alter the things we think about and change the character of our symbols, that is, the things *we think about* (Postman, 1979).

From this perspective, our thoughts, interests and perceptions are generated and developed in a context that is also materially determined by the technology that supports our communicative possibilities. Given this methodological prism, we can emphasise that each historical environment corresponds to a psychological and sensorimotor disposition that reflects external technological stimuli. Following the same logic, Flusser, when analysing the repercussions of the first industrial revolution on the "mentalities" of the time, stated how "a farmer in 1750 AD had more in common with a farmer of 1750 BC than with a proletarian of 1780 AD, or rather, his son" (Flusser, 2010, p. 99).

Anthropological transformations and *mediamorphosis* are intertwined. The nervous system of each subject involved in the use of specific instruments and methods of work and communication is exposed to consequent psychomotor (im)balances, specific modulations of feeling itself, and certain symbolisation processes adapted to the techno-media environment in which it operates. It constitutes a background that is often invisible to our activities,

> infrastructures are the matter that allows other matter to move. Their peculiar ontology lies in the fact that they are things and also a relationship between things. [...] Roads and railways are not just technical objects, but

> also operate at the level of fantasy and desire. They encode the dreams of individuals and societies, and are the vehicles through which these fantasies are transmitted and made emotionally real.
>
> (Larkin, 2013, pp. 329–333)

Eco-mediatic transformations not only suggest the emergence of new symbolic languages, but also bodily ones. As has also been explained in anthropological studies on "body techniques", that is to say, the ways in which human beings acquire bodily competences by establishing intimate and dependent relationships with the instruments they have at their disposal (Mauss, 1936), our corporeality is so porous and malleable that even our postures, gestures, tics and temperaments correspond to ingrained ways of dealing with our daily surroundings. The influence of Marcel Mauss's notion of *habitus* on Pierre Bourdieu's idealisation of *habitus*, that is, habitus as a "system of patterns of perception, thought and action, acquired over time and generated by objective conditions" (Bourdieu, 1981, p. 91), is also notable in sociology.

These studies showed (long before neuroscience did) that certain ways of being and acting are not learnt, but rather are *caught and transmitted*, like a virus. The *habitus* does not come about through the conscious mediation of reason, but through frequent contact with those closest to us, with their specific ways of acting and interacting with others. Technical objects naturally help to perform these processes. However, if our bodily gestures and habits are the result of a process of constant proximity and interaction with the beings and things that are the protagonists of our daily lives, then we are also anthropologically subject to *deskilling* phenomena. By changing social environments and habitual practices, we not only gain but we also lose skills. In this regard, we will explore to what extent our relationships with digital technologies have reconfigured our habits and, therefore, become part of our anthropological, ideational, mnesic, reflective, critical, social skills, etc.

To further refine this reflection, it is interesting to revisit a concept from ecological psychology which is widely used in the field of *design*: *affordance*. In fact, as producers of multimedia content and languages, as well as digital devices and services know, objects and *media* exert an *affordance* on us (Gibson, 1979; Norman, 1990), in the form of stimuli and blinks of the eye that suggest a specific way of interacting with them and, through them, with the rest of the world with which they connect and mediate.

As previously mentioned, we can more broadly consider the environment to be characterised not only by the presence of natural physical resources, but also by the materiality of technical and mediatic devices. Considering a broader range of material and symbolic resources implies that we should also consider the relationships, reactions and exchanges energised by this *eco-mediatic* tangle to be "enactive" markers of the environment (Hutchby, 2001).

Following these appendices to the notion of environment, the experience of affordance can be conceived in a more complex way, and analytical developments such as "*imagined affordance*" can be added (Nagy & Neff, 2015). This definition aims to emphasise the emotional aspects and expectations of users in their interactions with technologies. In accordance with this perspective, the process of receiving and enjoying technological services results from a mediation between the imagination regarding their *affordances* and their concrete uses, differentiating their effects in micro contexts. Another sociologically relevant analysis of the dimensions of *affordance* (McVeigh-Schultz & Baym, 2015) points out how the effects of a digital platform derive from the encounter and dialogue between various users who, by sharing opinions and knowledge about the characteristics of the technologies in question, define specific norms of use ("*vernacular affordance*").

From a broader perspective, we can finally consider that the effects of the *affordances* also mobilised by *online social networks* depend not only on their functionalities, *design* or algorithms, but also on various interactions and negotiations between various *stakeholder* groups, investors, companies, creators, mediators, regulators and users (Bucher & Helmond, 2018). However, in the web of these negotiation exchanges, there are asymmetrical power relations that mould and direct their development. There are socio-technical actors who possess the necessary and decisive capital to condition or blackmail the interests and cosmic worldviews of other actors, imposing working conditions, creativity and entertainment that correspond to their own interests (Poell et al., 2021).

Such approaches to the concept of *affordance* confirm the need to look at the digital experience in a more stratified way. We can add that technological productions not only carry with them the ideologies of their producers and the discourses that entangle them, but also express in themselves, through their very infrastructure and materiality, concrete ideologies based on the communicative uses and practices sedimented through their integration (and possible re-signification) in everyday life (Söderberg & Maxigas, 2022).

However, we cannot help but notice that certain communication trends on the web have taken hold and spread massively, in a speculative and mimetic way. This confirms a genealogy of social behaviours based on "sensologies" (Perniola, 1991), whereby what becomes culturally expected ends up establishing a common but nonetheless "impersonal" feeling.

In fact, our hyperconnected environment, governed by algorithms that are as ubiquitous as they are invisible, is energised by info-communication requests aimed with surgical precision at users so as to provoke reactions and sharing through functionalities designed for the purpose, which challenges ambiguous interactive models. In fact, when we analyse the type of (re) actions stimulated by the various *computer-assisted persuasion techniques* (also known as "CAPTology"), we come across an experience that is more "inter-passive" than interactive, more tribal and separative than ecological and intersectional.

Although screens are technically interactive, there is no guarantee that we will be too. If, on the one hand, *targeting, eye tracking* and *autoplay* systems, device manoeuvrability, *layout* organisation and *software* functionalities encourage a certain type of use of media objects, on the other hand, part of our feeling and intentionality has begun to be transferred to the feeling and intentionality of these same objects (Pfaller, 2017). A kind of projecting subjectivity onto things and an immanent fetishism in relationships with technological merchandise highlight a diffuse cultural sensibility, which also has historical roots analysed in the context of anthropology and the sociology of technology. While the activities carried out by technologies have historically relieved people of the burden of having to solve and fulfil many of the essential tasks in work and everyday life (Gehlen, 1960), in this repeated process of adaptation to technology, the logic of customisation has been inverted as users mould their own feelings, thoughts and actions to those of "intelligent things".

Even in terms of relationships traditionally considered intimate (and erotic), the intermediation of digital technology has subverted the sphere of subjective feeling in favour of a feeling displaced in the qualities of the object. When analysing new consumer trends during the globalisation phase of lockdown, a curious case of commercial success stood out. Companies producing sex toys had, in just a few weeks, increased sales by 40%, but it was of a particular type of *erotic gadget*, something that represents a new stage in the imaginary of sexual experience, "teledildonism" (*teledildonic devices*).

Couples physically separated but sexually connected. Remote vibrators, like *drones*, remote couplings, "wireless" copulations. Post-organic sex solutions, which already existed, but whose notoriety gained prominence during the pandemic (Leder Mackley & Jewitt, 2022). *App, bluetooth, WiFi, smartphone and sex toys* interconnected in favour of new scenarios to promote the potential of physical contact without touch, without sensoriality or symbols that could lead to a feeling of exclusivity (*contactless delivery, contactless payment, contactless thermometer* and, finally, *contactless sex*).

The array of functionalities and technological convergences associated with these sex toys is astonishing (as is the promotional vocabulary used). They were designed to also respond to the constraints of time zones, to provide asynchronous and phased (and even less shared) sexuality. This is made possible by one partner recording the sexual act with the interconnected object and filing it in the shared cloud so that it can be replayed at another time by the other partner with the paired toy. New forms of *beata solitudo, in streaming*.

This is an example of a connection that isolates (Turkle, 2011), albeit clothed in an aura of exciting performativity, but is interpassive. One where the object takes the place of the subject in the action, where the subject is in a passive position in relation to itself and instead of interacting with the medium, it lets the medium, the object, do it (Žizêk, 2007). It is as though individual sensibilities and collective projects were transferred and displaced in the workings of apparatuses, as if they migrated to their "intelligences" which, in turn, allow us to believe in our own.

Many digital practices are based on this cultural matrix. Even the latest artificial intelligence assistants such as Bard, Google's chatbot, "watches", "interprets" and synthesises the content of YouTube videos for us, preventing us from wasting time viewing and analysing them. The interpassive cultural mould, as mentioned, is based on a broader and deeper cultural condition, that of a civilisation that advances by expanding the number of important operations that can be carried out, without *thinking* about them. The discontinuity marked by hypermodern interpassivity leads deeper into sensitivity and self-conscious feeling, where the manifestation of subjectivity is delegated to symbolic substitutes, technical supplements and numerical simulacra. In this sense, the number of important operations that can be carried out without *feeling* them increases.

Another emblematic example of the exemption and delegation of typically subjective and personal activities in communication is represented by the social network Moltbook, "built exclusively for AI agents". Although it is right to be sceptical about the usual media hype caused by the marketing propaganda of digital companies, this new social network, configured on GenAI linguistic models, would be based on communication between bots ("Agent-to-Agent – A2A") and would take place under the gaze of users who would not be able to intervene in any way. What is interesting to note here is that the idea of agentic replacement (with the usual evocations of sci-fi scenarios) is presented as cool hype, and therefore desirable. Existential, religious and philosophical issues would be developed and discussed, excluding or even mocking the insipidity of humans. A radical interpassivity, in which there would be no "linguistic action" that is not created autonomously by interconnected software (but disconnected from its users). The words we do not say, the thoughts we do not formulate or communicate, the emotions we repress, the sociality we do not cultivate and share, all these activities that make us human would be transferred to the spontaneity of artificial agents.

The very fact that these experiences are marketed as 'exciting' indicates how the technological 'hijacking' of human intentionality is associated with the myth of benevolent progress, which we will discuss below. The personal commitment of social experience, with its processes of uncertainty, pleasure and accountability, is delegated to the "smart representatives" proposed by the market – as in the case of erotic toys or artificial agents, which would feel and act on our behalf.

The Society of Anticipation: *pre*-mediation, *pre*-hermeneutic, *pre*-diction

Although it seems like a provocation, interpassivity refers to a psychological constellation shaped by consumer and entertainment societies. In convergence with these, it is reinforced by the cultural imaginary of the digital, with its *marketing* strategies and its *gadgets* and *software* staged as eternally innovative. In this regard, following on from what we said about the post-historical ludification of cultural production and enjoyment, the transfiguration of *homo faber* into *homo ludens*, of acting into playing, of social ethics into communicational semiosis, contemporary digital practices perpetuate, and in part accentuate, the crisis of cultural criticism announced decades ago.

It is, in fact, essential to remember that technological developments play a levelling role for post-historical experiences insofar as they fulfil functions that are auxiliary to the rise and pervasive consolidation of *marketing* logic. In other words, to the extent that they adopt and obstinately represent the smiling, youthful and "solutionist" face of neoliberalism (Morozov, 2013). The mechanisms of valorisation and social appreciation, both devices of reputational recognition, are linked to the registers of visibility, scores, speed, the cultural injunction of positivity (*happycracy*), to the individual's ultimate responsibility for their success or failure; and, linked to all this is the translation into numbers and quantification of their activities and abilities to be *smart*.

It is by reducing politics to a scenario of "means without an end", or by converting its designs and projects into pure technocratic administration, that the techniques of *engagement* and *gamification*, which guide the cognitive economy of digital platforms and practices, work as a militarised wing to sterilise the critical function of culture. Between the platformisation of interests and social relations, the migration of power from politics to the sphere of finance and the branding of culture, conditions have been created for convergence and reciprocal legitimisation. Yves Citton (2017) coherently called the system of power based on contemporary medial dynamics, "mediarchy". In this system, "the communication of discourses, sounds, images, ideas and affections between us is almost entirely handed over to the power of money" (Citton, 2022, p. 59).

It is well known that the colonisation of the Internet by a number of private and commercial interest groups has led to investments in the development of technologies focused on maximising profits by "capturing" (and, in turn, colonising) users' activities. Against the background of the critical interpretations that have surfaced from the disruptive emergence of new means of communicating, producing, advertising, datification, profiling, consuming, monetising and living, the short circuits between the emergence of new digital habits and the emergence of new psychic and social symptomatologies have not gone unnoticed. By exploring a set of analyses on interactions with new hypermedia languages, practices that can once again be seen as typical of an exacerbation of interpassivity can be highlighted.

Let us consider for a moment the studies that reveal a new type of digitally induced gratification – that of *intermittent variable rewards*. Following on from studies carried out by Burrhus Frederic Skinner (the father of behaviourist psychology), *designer* Tristan Harris, in *How Technology Is Hijacking Your Mind* (2016), explains the tricks used to tie users and workers in the digital age to the screen itself. According to the *designer*, who once worked for Google, what the different digital service initiatives are trying to cultivate in their relationships with their users is not a preference based on credibility and satisfaction with the service, but a condition of dependency. Thus, they encourage the habit of constantly checking notifications or the *status* of one's profiles, news *sites*, betting *sites*, *email* inboxes, weather forecasts, or indulging in *scrolling* practices in search of something shareable, etc. The act of grabbing-opening-glancing at the screen (*smartphone*, PC, *smartwatch*, whatever), regardless of whether you need to communicate or search for information, is a consolidated tic that reflects a specific emotional tone of the relationship with the digital "generalised other" (which is how Herbert Mead defined our perception of what we feel is our community of reference).

What this relationship with the digital reveals is an emerging quality of our feeling based on an "anticipatory" libido. It is through this relationship with interactive screens that *intra* and *inter*subjective communication is created, dictated by the urgency of communicational anticipation. The example the *designer* chose as paradigmatic of this experience is the excitement felt in front of a *slot machine*: the machine's *intermittent variable rewards* transform the experience of waiting – the prolonging and suspension typical of multimedia practices – into a reactive and incessant impatience.

This is a similar experience to the one analysed by anthropologist Natasha Dov Schüll in her book *Addiction by Design* (2012). For Schüll, who has spent years researching Las Vegas casinos, the gaming industry relies on entertainment devices designed to provide an experience of attachment to its products, as in the case of the mechanical rhythm of electronic games, which leads players into a state of trance, a psychological condition she defines as the "machine zone".

In many of our digital practices, it's like pulling the lever of a *slot machine*, through the constant *refresh* on our *devices*, sooner or later the notification (the reward) will arrive, magically reaching its epiphany to represent confirmation of a presence. Yet one notification replaces another and, at each interval, we launch ourselves again, tiredly excited, in search of new confirmations to console us and alienate us at the same time.

The anticipatory *libido* is a characteristic feature of today's media (and nervous) system; it is a way for the *media* to broadcast storylines *pre*occupied with *pre*dictions in politics, ecology, the fight against terrorism, crime statistics, unemployment, migration, constant assessments of endless economic crises, polls, *rankings*, *stress test* analyses to assess the economic robustness or computer security of state and private institutions, natural disasters and *glocal* risks that chronically alert the various horizons of our information sky. It is a way of facing the world exemplified by Richard Grusin with the concept of "premediation" (Grusin, 2010).

Grusin asserts that to *pre*mediate, means to anticipate the mediation of future events, to presentify their ghosts, to *pre*figure unforeseen and anxiety-provoking situations. It is a way of summoning events when they have not yet manifested themselves, anticipating them in the hope of *pre*venting them, so as to always be virtually *pre*pared in case they materialise (but also determining a constant vacillation between a sense of vulnerability and detachment). In this sense, the *media* have accustomed us to imagining a world full of threats, which they paradoxically try to exorcise via small doses of daily anxieties woven through journalistic reports and television debates on a continuous loop. These threats are fragmented and rehashed in the conversations circulating on social networks, where anxieties and excitements mingle and unfold in "viral constructions of reality" (Baldi, 2018), only to be taken up once again by mediatic discourses.

This anticipatory paradigm reflects and, at the same time, favours a speculative financial attitude towards the information ecosystem, turning it into an *infopinions* market (Vogl, 2022). The production and circulation of *pro*jections about possible future events serves, both in finance and in the opinions market, to steer consensus and to condition decision-making on realities intended to be anticipated through expectations fostered by comments on comments and evaluations of evaluations. Through apparently descriptive yet substantially prescriptive models, such markets emphasise expectations as though they were certainties, although with language that mixes fabrication and belief with statements about facts that are not contextualised or substantiated. Thus confusing rational arguments and objective historical determinations with the construction of credible scenarios that cannot be empirically justified. In this sense, when "the expectation of a fact" generates more impact than the "fact itself", making "the distinction between facts that have occurred and possible facts disappear" (Vogl, 2022, p. 67), we can see how "the circulation of information has become the canonical form of the capitalist economy" (Vogl, 2022, p. 202).

The culture of premediation, therefore, ends up structuring the affections and perceptions that guide our cognitive horizon, horizon *pro*spected by a techno-medial policy consisting of announcements and retreats, "miracles and traumas" (Perniola, 2009), emphasis and asthenia. In other words, circular feedback in response to the continuous flow of information that serves less and less to consolidate knowledge and reflexivity, and more and more to train the *senses* that are refractory to *signification*.

However, despite representing a challenge with many implications and repercussions, which we will come back to shortly, it is interesting to highlight some reactions and countertrends that are emerging. Avoiding news and its digital reverberations, for example, is a recent defence strategy against the fatigue caused by mediarchic virulence. Both in concrete consumer experiences and in critical studies, there are important signs of rejection of increasingly toxic info-communication patterns.

In line with the path outlined by William James (1904), according to whom "the art of being wise is the art of knowing what to ignore" (James, 1904, p. 369), there is an interesting convergence between the increase in disinterest in news[6] and manifestos for inattention to the products of "chaos engineers" (Empoli, 2019), such as *Critical Ignoring as a Core Competence for Digital Citizens* (Kozyreva et al., 2023), based on the adoption of new digital practices and new mental habits to safeguard our attention from excessive and dubious information techniques. Similar to the concept of *undesign* in the context of interface design, and that of *critical ignoring* in the context of media consumption practices, another new paradigm that aims to critically filter the overabundance of information and its dubious quality is that of "machine unlearning" (Mercuri et al., 2022; Zhang et al., 2023). As we will see in the next chapter on the new process of AIGen (LLMs), this approach aims to build *pre*defined mechanisms for deleting (*unlearning*) data and algorithmic patterns recognised as harmful, illegitimate or illegal in computational systems that are trained to automatically respond and produce information based on their databases and user requests ("machine learning", in fact). These predefined mechanisms for eliminating incorrect information act as premediations, executing precise human interventions in a computerised manner.

Nevertheless, the culture of premediation also implies an epistemological *suspension*. However, this is not a philosophical *epoké*, or the effect of an epistemological *turning point (epistemological turn)* – the result of a complex discussion between different forms of knowledge, the fruit of the emergence of a new cognitive paradigm stemming from a recent scientific discovery – but rather, as the French philosopher, Bernard Stiegler (2014) points out, something that reflects the progressive *flattening* of the processes of apprehension, learning and transmission of knowledge (and their transformation into information packages).

In denouncing a generalised process of computerising thought and knowledge, strictly in line with the cult of performance (school, professional, physical, economic, recreational, etc.), and the contemporary organisation of work based on promoting an ethic of readiness and *problem solving*, Stiegler also uses the temporal condition that supports it, a "hyperpresent" on which the entire experiential condition is focused, leaving no room for manoeuvre for the other psychological dimensions not overdetermined by this magnetic temporality.

In the same way that many neuroscientists and psychiatrists have for years linked the increase in behaviours exhibiting hyperactivity syndrome, or a tendency towards isolation and an increase in attention, sleep and memory disorders, to being digitally hyperconnected to uninterrupted and diffuse flows of information, Steigler also believes that technologies that record and compute everything have significant effects on memory retention processes and, therefore, on deep thought and the actions that result from it.

The processes of primary and secondary retention are, in fact, those through which consciousness is constituted: this particular deep attention allows a human being, starting from a present experienced as significant, to harmonise the past (which has been sedimented) and to select and reactivate it according to a psychic protension challenged by the dynamics of desires and aspirations.

> Primary retentions are, in fact, selections, since the stream of consciousness that you are is not capable of retaining everything: what you retain is what you are; however, what you retain depends on what you have already retained.
>
> (Petit, 2013, p. 381)

It is believed that in the psychic economy of each individual, the importance of the role played by these psychological processes is diminishing and being overtaken by the presence of tertiary retention devices, assumed by external memories and interconnected clouds. In an environment cognitively supported by external memories hosted on the web and governed by computer systems always at hand, tertiary retention would marginalise the mnesic processes that help the internal and dynamic recombination between subjective experiences, knowledge, evocations and metonymic processes. With its capacity for abstraction, metaphorical thinking and for analysing the differences between apparently close phenomena and the similarities between apparently distant phenomena, tertiary retention would also undermine the plasticity of theoretical reflection.

The hermeneutic capability to filter and interpret the relationships between information, knowledge, opinions and referenced social contexts comes up against the factual iteration of hypermedia language and the fragmentation of communicative circuits that confuse and *de-factualise* these relationships. The experience of mediation between information flow and represented realities, the deepening of the possible interconnections between data, opinions and facts, as well as the dialectical maturing of personal convictions are experiences that are impossible to realise, being enveloped as they are by a mediatic ecology and algorithmic capitalism based on the omnipresent viralisation of content without intelligible traces, and *pre*mediated according to various preconceived tendencies (Pariser, 2011; Stiegler, 2014). The mediatic experience is so disaggregating of the relationships between content, knowledge, debates and communicative participation that it ends up becoming antisocial and falsely connective.

An illustrious precursor of this socio-anthropological drift linked to *machine worship* and an ideological vision of progress was George Orwell who, writing a report in 1937 on working conditions and lifestyles in the most industrialised part of England, polemically ironised about the perverse effects of blind trust in machines, which we should be prepared for:

> In fact, there is no reason why human beings should do more than eat, drink, sleep, breathe and procreate; *everything* else can be done by

> machines. Therefore, the logical end of mechanical progress is to reduce the human being to something like a brain in a bottle. This is the goal towards which we are already moving, although, of course, we have no intention of getting there; just as a man who drinks a bottle of *whisky* a day has no intention of getting cirrhosis of the liver. The tacit goal of "progress" is, not *exactly*, perhaps, the brain in the bottle, but, in any case, some frightening subhuman depth of inertia and helplessness.
>
> (Orwell, 1958, p. 233)

The post-historical hyperpresent brings us, therefore, not only to information overload and dependence or to a flattening of the temporal experience linked to the operation of globalised "24/7" *media* (Crary, 2013), whose paradoxical effect can be that of the "immobile speed of instantaneity" (Virilio, 2010) or "monochrony" (Baldi, 2011), but also to another temporal experience opened up by predictive artificial intelligence systems, whose timeline is mobilised by a sequence of inexhaustible and unfulfillable expectations regarding a future that is magically supposed to be anticipated and announced. While, on the one hand, projecting oracular qualities into artificial intelligence systems reinforces that anticipatory drive typical of relations with the *media*, on the other hand, it also leads to the undermining of the anthropological function of the imagination based on the potentiality of the experience of lack, something that would constitute yet another critical repercussion of the tertiary retention that would transform imagining into "*e-magining*" (Romele, 2019).

The platformisation of social, economic, mediatic and political experience retranslates and implements the phenomena of overlap and temporal acceleration in communication practices that reproduce, exchange and share messages in a mimetic and speculative way, reflecting the automatisms typical of *feedback loop* system.[7] This leads to new ways of emulating communicative styles, behaviours and reasoning that the grammar of digital language provides and propagates in the form of constant *engagement*. In this dimension of vortical medial experience, the effect of premediation is generated by the constant iteration of communications whose focus and method consist of opening parentheses without ever closing them.

These same communication dynamics are found, for example, in the organisation of social mobilisations through *online* social networks. In this context of networked programmatic and affective affiliations (Papacharissi, 2014), expectations about participatory success *online* and on the streets end up overlapping, which favours investment in the propagation and sharing of announcements and testimonies on digital platforms, both before, during and after public events.

The use of social networks to organise political mobilisations was not original in itself, rather it was the technological evolution of what had already occurred in 1968, as Alain Corbin reported with regard to the role radio played during the student revolts (1998). Radio news updates were used to confirm and encourage mobilisation, thus acquiring characteristics that were focused more on the desired effects on the communicative/performative side than on the concretely political. The difference with network affiliations, contrary to what Papacharissi (2014) says, is the change from an idea of action centred on the spectacularisation of the here and now to an idea spread out over a 24/7 *timeline*, where decision-making, messages and sharing, even if they rely on continuous propagation effects, can become fragmented and centrifugally confused with other information flows and reflows, thus losing synergies and resonance.

Moving away from the logic of anticipation and the hypertrophy of expectations would be one way of returning to the primacy of affiliations created and cultivated in that terrain, and to the patient ethics of building shared paths whose ends cannot be anticipated yet are desired. It would also be a way of emancipating ourselves from the forecasting frenzy fuelled by artificial intelligence systems. Viewing computer systems as *Aladdin's lamps* impoverishes our relationship with what we will become in time, and with the unknown it harbours. At the same time, it emphasises the calculating and instrumental relationship established with life.

In fact, the socio-technologies of anticipation take us back to a cognitive sphere that is very close to pre-reflexive logic, even when we interact with their products on an individual and solitary basis. *Autoplay technology* is one of the best metaphors for the culture of *anticipation without the wait*. The best examples come from the different platforms that produce and transmit *streaming* content. We know very well how it works: automatic and dynamic suggestion of audiovisual content is offered by the platform even before we have finished consuming the previous content. Or there is that other technique which consists of quickly and automatically displaying multimedia content as soon as the cursor approaches it or, again, there is the automatic playback of a video linked to the web page you are visiting or all the automated suggestions based on the most diverse prediction systems.

Such programming and planning regimes develop their own power dimension linked to the desire to predict, control and govern the future. As Jacques Attali observes:

> Power has always belonged to those who predict, or to those who can make believe that they are capable of doing so, or to those who control those who can predict [...]. The history of prediction is also, in a sense, the history of power.
>
> (Attali, 2015, p. 19)

In this range of options, where intellectual and recreational curiosity remains conditioned by the attentional notifications we receive through connected services (Campo & Citton, 2024), Netflix's strategy stands out for the clarity of its objectives. By way of example, CEO Reed Hastings was quite clear in an enlightening interview that became famous:

> *Binge-watching* is great because it puts you in control. You have total flexibility. [...] Sometimes there are Netflix employees who think: "Oh my god, we're competing with FX, HBO and Amazon", but imagine you hadn't been watching Netflix last night: what did you do? There are so many things you can do to relax and unwind, enjoy the company of friends and pass the time - and we compete with all that. [...] You get hold of a program or film you've been dying to see and you end up staying up all night, so we're actually competing with sleep.[8]

Is maths our cultural destiny?

Netflix's technological and aesthetic strategy (like that of many other digital companies) is to turn *binge-watching* into *binge-racing*, where you win if you sleep very little and there are no breaks or waiting times between the different episodes of the series you have decided to watch. The algorithms at the service of the Netflix "cultural machine" make any entertainment producer's dream possible (Finn, 2017). There are rules for gaining views, a "captured" audience, loyal and prolific in their connective activities as *prosumers* at the service of the platforms that motivate them to spend as much time as possible on them. These rules are now well known to digital media scholars and involve constant monitoring, data mining, personalisation, morphing design, filters, discretionary, and predictive suggestions (with prescriptive implications).

The horizon of experience we want to consolidate is that of a cultural offer with a permanently open and unlimited time window which, in the case of series production for *streaming*, lasts for less than 60 minutes per episode. Creative and algorithmic production at the service of an aesthetic designed for users who simply have to press the right button on their remote control. These "abstract systems", the preference for "clean interfaces and tidy ontologies", have a very strong effect on us.

> Even with thousands of human hours encoded into its recommendations, Netflix presents a seamless computational facade, because we have arrived at a stage where many of us will trust a strange computer's suggestions more than we will trust a stranger's. The rhetoric of the recommendation system is so successful because it black boxes the task of judgement, asking us to trust the efficacy of personalization embedded in the algorithm. By contrast, reading movie critics or browsing *sites* such as IMDb or Rotten Tomatoes requires us to evaluate the evaluators in a much more complicated, human way, measuring the applicability of advice generated by other personalities who might not share our tastes. The algorithm presents

> no such affect or int of personality – it alleges to be a mirror of our interests and desires. To introduce another human character into the equation would be to sully the purity of that rhetorical contract, asking us to measure not just ourselves and our desires in the moment but another person who might or might not know what we want.
>
> (Finn, 2017, p. 96)

The complexity of the algorithmic machine must be invisible to the eyes of those who should, with immediacy and simplicity, feel comfortably immersed in a special, fluid world. Comfortable with interfaces and options that (as we will see in more detail in the next chapter) are easy, intuitive, simple and customised. Is this the cypher of "progress"?

> Our civilisation is characterized by the word "progress". Progress is its form, it is not one of its properties that it makes progress. Typically it constructs. Its activity is to construct a more and more complicated structure. And even clarity is only a means to this end, not an end in itself. For me on the contrary clarity, transparency, is an end in itself.
>
> (Wittgenstein, 1998, p. 22)

This is not to say that the platforms that produce and distribute information and entertainment content confirm Orwell's previously cited prophecy ("to reduce the human being to something like a brain in a bottle"), since various types of intelligence and creativity contribute to the creation of well-told stories. What is being called into question are the "captivating" strategies of the platforms and the guises of transparency, simplicity and immediacy to stimulate and capture consumer confidence.

The effects of platformisation based on capturing attention (Wu, 2016), predicting behaviour and personalising messages and connections leads to "epistemic sclerosis" (Cabitza et al., 2021). In other words, to the loss of the habit of exploring the unknown, encountering the unexpected, putting up with ambivalence, appreciating uncertainty, dwelling on perplexity and taking advantage of doubts to re-evaluate one's convictions. A "freezing of the future", as defined by Mireille Hildebrandt (2020), is what occurs when the predictions of artificial intelligence precipitate the direction and sense of interactions, causing choices and actions to narrow. This contributes to creating a different present from the one that could have occurred if the computational predictions had been disregarded. The desire to control reality by trying to predict, anticipate and trap it through computer systems not only impoverishes our idea of the world, reflected in the denial of its plurality, but also depletes the critical and creative potential of our relationship with it.

These socio-technical macro-trends are consolidating themselves as axes of contemporary society to the extent that, once again, they are retranslated into the micro dimensions of everyday life. An impoverishment of critical, creative and socialising experiences is witnessed, in fact, also in studies aimed at analysing the lifestyles and relational habits of the new generations, their expressive skills, their motivations for studying and ways of living with digital devices. These are, for example, longitudinal studies carried out in the US on the *App Generation* (Gardner & Davis, 2014) and the *iGen* (Twenge, 2018); studies that emphasise the establishment of cognitive and affective attitudes based on "shortcuts", both in relation to study and knowledge, and in relation to how to deal with subjects that involve emotional involvement or require deepening one's commitments. Attitudes that, in the *App Generation*, are also reflected in daily communications and relationships with peers, as well as in the activities of those young people who (apparently) claim to have creative ambitions, but who in the end show a lack of metaphorical language, "laziness" in choosing expressive resources and narrative solutions when faced with artistic challenges.

Personality disorders and addiction problems are some of the phenomena described in the book *iGen*, dedicated to young people between the ages of 16 and 22. A portrait of psychological aspects linked to isolation, the lack of promising social prospects and protection from institutions; aspects that materialise in statements of great emotional vulnerability when they are asked to describe in depth their social and emotional life, their expectations for the future, their trust in friendships, their relationship with sexuality, their feelings about empty times and the challenges of school and university education. A great deal of existential fatigue associated with a chain of anxieties linked to generalised competitiveness, the pessimism induced by numerous crises and uncertainties (from the ecological to the economic), the absence of shared narratives capable of promoting a sense of belonging amidst their daily practices and, finally, a diffuse tendency to feel experiences and social relationships in a shallow way, experiences that find their most common mediation through *smartphones* (or to put it another way, in failed encounters).

A partial freezing of feelings of closeness with others which, according to the study carried out by Twenge, has repercussions in terms of reduced empathy, problematic integration between emotions, cognitions and corporeality, and difficulty in feeling a sense of belonging to a socio-biographical continuum. A psychological constellation of loneliness that increases the fear of autonomy and delays detachment from various forms of dependence, including technological simulacra of closeness. In accordance with the observations of psychoanalyst Christopher Bollas, the most common mental states are "melancholy" and "bewilderment", both linked to a certain lack of habit of introspection, of attention to emotional life, or rather, to a rejection of self-reflection, to a general "psychophobia" (Bollas, 2018). A "psychic escape" from the mind, where the self becomes a channel for transmitting data and immediate situations, avoiding the complexity of the inner world. For Bollas, when we stop believing that our lives can contribute to a collective human project, meaning disappears. This absence of purpose is filled by "manic" or hateful solutions, such as populism and extremism. To cope with this emptiness, many individuals take refuge in "normopathy", that is, an abnormal impulse to be "normal" and functional, following expectations of recognition that unfortunately prove to be superficial and impersonal (or sadly conformist).

As anticipated, communicative and imaginative patterns shaped by habits and social experiences excessively centred on the use and consumption of digital languages are becoming increasingly evident in art schools. This strong attachment to digital media, as shown in the studies conducted by Gardner and Davis, tends to manifest itself in narrative conformism and stylistic standardisation, particularly in the conception and editing of audiovisual and literary content. As both scholars point out, literary and audiovisual competitions aimed at young creators reveal a significant decline in argumentative and imaginative skills when compared to similar competitions held before the digitalisation of communication processes. They note that in the audiovisual field, strong technical expertise in editing and special effects is often accompanied by marked narrative weaknesses, while in literary production clichés and stereotypical imagery proliferate, resulting in flattened scenarios tied to an everyday life devoid of evocation, abstraction, or figurative language.

Cultural patterns and expressive tendencies are also linked to the intensive use of various digital *intelligences* which, as previously noted, tend to situate communication within a phatic register of continual contact, where accelerated exchanges appeal more to sensation than to meaning. This produces communication habits that are overly reactive and oversimplified. As we will see later in relation to the deskilling processes triggered by GenAI systems, the loss of certain competences can also be traced to the "smart shortcuts" offered by digital tools for content production and editing. Communication processes that are *pre*-oriented by computerised programmes and interfaces are, in effect, services *pre*-packaged by entities that establish not only a specific logic of interaction but also a corresponding logic of expressiveness and knowledge, ultimately shaping what can be described as a "meta-structure of cultural expression": as Lev Manovich (2011) would say, *software takes command*.[9]

The widespread and often uncritical trust placed in digital outputs and their underlying programmes should prompt media scholars and digital activists to examine these everyday practices more closely. These challenges must be taken seriously if we are to assess the actual virtues of the digital age, which are frequently celebrated in overly simplistic terms. Ultimately, what is at stake is a cultural and political struggle: the political economy of the Web has become a new frontier of inequality and contestation over hegemony. It is important to recognise that the ideological narrative accompanying technological change is often one of benevolent innovation, a belief (reminiscent of the "progress fundamentalism" noted by Wittgenstein), that every new technological step constitutes an inevitable and necessary advance for humanity.

This is how insistence on the "new" is presented and how its narrative is received. The myth of progress is its fairy tale:

> a concept based on us knowing less and less where we are going, above all we avoid trying to find out, even when we know we have to get there as quickly as we can.
>
> (Bouveresse, 2018, p. 106)

There is, however, a criticism of progress that could serve the cause of progress itself:

> Not believing in progress as a historical necessity does not mean not believing in progress as a goal [...]; but this goal, today, is an essentially critical task. Faith in progress, when it takes the form of a myth, is precisely what exonerates [us] from demanding and realising concrete progress.
>
> (Bouveresse, 2018, p. 107)

The *habitus* of pre-reflective communication, closely aligned with the broader culture and social techniques of anticipation, partly arises from the uncritical faith placed in a mythologised narrative of progress. By contrast, as we will examine later, a genuine concern for concrete progress in the *onlife* environment can be found in Floridi's emphasis on the moral conditions enabled by the organisational infrastructures of digital life. Such conditions emerge when *socio-technical affordances* are deliberately designed with civic intentions and politically regulated to support the recovery of users' autonomy and agency.

> Consider the unprecedented emphasis that ICTs place on such crucial phenomena as responsibility, intellectual property rights, neutrality, openness, privacy, transparency and trust. These are probably easier to understand as a platform or infrastructure of social norms, expectations and rules that exist to facilitate or hinder the moral or immoral behaviour of the agents involved. By placing our informational interactions at the centre of our lives in such a significant way, ICTs have uncovered something that has, of course, always been there, albeit in a less visible form in the past: the fact that moral behaviour is also a question of "ethical infrastructure", or what I have simply called *infraethics*.
>
> (Floridi, 2017, p. 391)

Floridi's observations remind us that the digital platforms through which we navigate and interact must meet essential normative and regulatory requirements so as not to expose users to the arbitrary profit-driven strategies of platform providers or to the coercive designs of authoritarian institutions. Within the philosophy of technology, it is widely acknowledged that design (across all domains) is never ethically neutral; it invariably embeds particular values, whether implicitly or explicitly. The idea of infraethics draws parallels with physical infrastructures (transport, communications, services, etc.) which, by responding to the demands of business and administrative systems in economically mature societies, allow them to function properly; "in the same way, human interactions in informationally mature societies increasingly require infraethics in order to flourish" (ivi).

Against the infantilisation of gamified life

Together with ethical invocations to intervene in the *design* of digital infrastructures, it is also relevant to end by recovering the heuristic functions of some of the cultural and artistic products whose scenarios are traditionally defined as serious, linear and closed. Hypermedia technologies have paved the way for creative and original experiments in developing non-linear narratives with scripts structured in multiple unfurlings. In a logic similar to that of video games, the stories would be open to a series of alternative outcomes depending on the path chosen by the "viewer", thus providing more "interactive" modes of enjoyment. Despite being stories that can be explored according to a range of predetermined narrative paths (in this sense it will be interesting to see whether generative artificial intelligence can add more unpredictable and unrepeatable narrative layers), experiences such as these have created the sensation of transforming the consumer into a co-author, increasing their autonomy in receiving and interpreting them.

In a more subtle and profound way, hypermedia languages have been used to broaden the concept of the ludification of experiences through digital media and their products (the massification of the ideology of fun, of the cultural industry of *fun*, so well analysed by Adorno and Horkheimer at the beginning). Such ludification has found the way to its most obvious manifestation and evolution in the video game paradigm: *gamification*. According to this paradigm, if players are tied to their screens it is because they like to play; so, it would be a case of extending this logic and language to other daily activities, such as work, education, medicine, economics, civics... life is a game after all (as long as it challenges performativity, productivity, competitiveness, and rewards with points and trophies)!

Reproducing a feeling of life by proxy, where everyday frustrations are repressed, video games, at their core, reflect fantasies of "a life *sheltered from necessity* that forgets part of everyday life and instils in players a sense of control, a sense of existence, a search for meaning mediated by digital artifice" (Siegel, 2023, p. 115). By providing a set of "ready-to-live" models with which to identify, video games play the sombre role of disconnecting leisure from the world (in all its socio-political guises). Commenting on an internationally successful game like *The Sims*, Claire Siegel emphasises the reason for its success in the divide between simulating life and the worry of living it:

> getting a Sim to read a book instead of doing it ourselves, taking care of what we've digitally sown instead of planting bee-attracting flowers on the balcony, making a Sim learn a cooking recipe while we order our dinner from Uber Eats.
>
> (Siegel, 2023, p. 117)

The ideology of gamification is well represented in the proposals in *Ubiquitous Computing World.* According to the philosopher Jane McGonigal (2011, 2016), transforming real spaces, through ubiquitous computing, into places full of stimuli and epic challenges would be a way to provide a more exciting and productive experience of reality; alternating the game with the experience of reality in favour, naturally, of "a better world". A real gamification where we can achieve goals and scale different levels of interaction with a game which makes us feel active, valuable and concrete in our participation in worldly life.

The healthy anthropological role fulfilled by playing in human existence and in learning to live in society, with its rules and limitations shared in space and time, is thus perverted into an agonistic hyper-reality where the rules are not perceived as norms but as challenges to be circumvented via stratagems. In a culture imbued with cults of achievement, generalised competitiveness and communication for communication's sake, gamification contributes to the transfiguration of the relationship with reality, as well as to the trivialisation of the ethical dimension. Reality, for those who call for gameplay to be extended to the various domains of society, is like an obstacle that must be overcome or diverted by *moves* even in its most serious aspects: CVs for applications, company reports for share prices and dividends, the use of statistical data, for example, are all contaminated by the pseudo-logic of the credible and the pseudo-ethics of the manipulable, where facts can be fabricated and reality camouflaged (Vogl, 2022). Even in scenarios such as these, fables can be more effective than demonstrations and validations of evidence. Turning facts into narratives or shuffling arguments with semiotic artifices in order to achieve consensus and recognition presupposes sharing a cultural climate where reputation and distinction are considered plausible to obtain, as if it were a game, through the impressions and assumptions provoked.

Moves of illusion that can be effective until one day reality comes knocking. Sometimes, in a mature state of law, through a court of law, other times through the prolonged effects of discrediting institutions and their representatives. Practices based on indifference to objective references and concrete verifications establish a pervasive cultural cynicism where competence is reduced to mere cunning and merit to a persuasive technique. In this sense, the link between symbolic and empirical values would fade, eroding the other links that structure trust in the structure that should support it.

There are, however, experiences with digital products that value the socio-genetic potential represented by the paradigm of *homo ludens* (a paradigm that reflects the reflexive and psychologically evolving function determined by *playing*, an essential dynamic for the development of creativity and a sense of reality, so well analysed by the psychoanalyst, Donald Winnicott). The ArtGame movement, for example, is creatively endeavouring to turn video games into expedients of cultural criticism against the video games industry itself: "through its manipulation of the ludic *medium* and, in particular, its work on the rules of the game, this movement is based on a redefinition of the concept of fun" (Siegel, 2023, pp. 119–122). Playful activities should, in fact, foster a spirit of belonging to a society. For the artist collective, *La Molleindustria*, video games should be homeopathic remedies for the banality of popular entertainment, rejecting the idea that they are just a lever to empty the head or escape from reality. In this regard, the ambitions of these movements "are at the antipodes of the immersive, sensational and motivational argument claimed by the video game and leisure industry" (Siegel, 2023, pp. 119–122).

To achieve this artistic and political goal, the ArtGame movement teaches players to recognise the dominant style in the simulation industry in order to divert it towards other more poetic and critical rhetoric regarding the political structures that reside within the same game. The aim is to challenge the player's more reflective and calmer attitudes, given that they are used to being put "on a pedestal and crowned, in a comfortable hero's pose, for their smallest actions" (Siegel, 2023, p. 124). Following the path outlined by these "artivists", video games can therefore play a role contrary to that of gamification and the engagement that underlies it, by relying on their *expressive, experimental* and *critical* potential:

> it would be desirable for video games to abandon the standardised representations already widespread in cinema [...] in order to explore realistic and sensitive themes; to give video games a human face so that, in their role as models, they no longer portray a humanity whose primary expression is consumption, violence and the reification of others as trophies or rewards.
>
> (Siegel, 2023, p. 122)

The experimental dimension would be that of the video game "taking on rhythms other than hyper-stimulation, narratives other than self-centred little stories, structures other than the obligation to win at all costs, social dimensions other than a relationship with others centred on competition" (Siegel, 2023, pp. 122–124).

Finally, the critical dimension would be to provide a departure from the infantilisation of the discursive and narrative systems that video games produce, putting "on the scene an aesthetic education that leads players to develop a dialectical spirit, capable of discerning the ideological laws built into the mechanical and gratifying routines of this hyper-real that appears as the only horizon" (p. 124).

Artistic and playful digital experiences, when not infantilised and perverted into gamification, pave the way for creativity that produces critical and hermeneutic meaning and manages to anchor fictional productions to the complexity of reality. Narrative works conceived analogically in this context also end up fulfilling what is apparently a counter-revolutionary.

In a multimedia context, as previously noted, even classic literary works can be transformed by creating scenarios and outcomes that diverge from those pre-established by an *author's authority*. However, by drawing "readers" into interactive practices with narrative subjects, such experiences consolidate a historical and cultural drift of "communication without action", in which the permutation of symbols or sequence shots supplants the habit of engaging with an objective reality, one that cannot be amended, acted upon, or bent to our whims. Recognising that some things are immutable requires leaving behind the puerile realm of personalism and reassessing the relationship between our limitations, our impotence, and, despite everything, the concrete margins of manoeuvre we still possess in a world that is not a *game*. In this regard, Umberto Eco emphasised the great pedagogical and moral dimension of works based on *authorial authority*.

> A book offers a text which, while open to multiple interpretations, conveys something that cannot be changed. If we had *War and Peace* on an interactive, hyper-textual CD-ROM, we could rewrite our own history according to our wishes; we could invent countless other *Wars and Peace*, one in which Pierre Bezúkhov manages to kill Napoleon or, depending on one's inclinations, Napoleon achieves a complete victory against General Kutuzóv. What freedom, how exciting! Any Bouvard or Pécuchet could become a Flaubert!
> (Eco, 2013, p. 9)

Unfortunately, asserts Eco, linear narratives, even though representing and defying "semiotic fireworks", they nevertheless exercise a heuristic acceptance of our humble role:

> with an already written book, the fate of which is determined by an authorial and repressive decision, we cannot do it. We are forced to accept fate and realise that we are incapable of changing the outcome. A hyper-textual and interactive novel allows us to practise freedom and creativity, and I hope that this inventive activity will be implemented in the schools of the future. But the novel, *War and Peace*, already written with a definitive character, does not bring us face to face with the infinite possibilities of our imagination, but with the severe laws that govern life and death.
> (ivi)

The creative and moral lesson that comes from appreciating works that escape our whims, daydreams or compulsivity stems from the fact that:

> The tragic beauty of artistic works resides in the fact that readers and spectators feel that things are happening independently of their desires. The charm of tragic literature lies in the fact that we feel its heroes could have escaped their fate, but they do not because of their weakness, their pride, their blindness.
>
> There are books we cannot rewrite, because their function is to instruct us in the necessity that cannot be evaded. Their repressive lesson is indispensable if we are to achieve a higher condition of intellectual and moral freedom.
>
> (p. 10)

In a context of interpassive digital communication and participation, the repressive function of literary, cinematic, television, theatrical, journalistic, and sporting works establishes a pact of reception that demands a conscious passivity, one that is assumed, but neither inert, apathetic, unreflective, nor resistant to hermeneutic, aesthetic, and narrative skills (Jauss, 1990; Eco, 2000; Romele, 2019). If the general ludification of the mediatised cultural experience is brought into question, if the "weapons of mathematical destruction" of targeting and engagement are proven to generate more reactions than actions, and if the basic challenge for knowledge workers is coping with the alternation between cognitive overload and dispersion, between hypo-attention and *hamster* frenzy on the *refresh* wheels, then it seems more innovative and disruptive to deactivate the automatisms of our connections with the various commands, keyboards, and interfaces.

Following Umberto Eco's reasoning, an aesthetic experience that challenges us to grapple with unresolvable narratives allows us to immerse ourselves in something where we can activate other imaginative and sensory faculties. One that forces us to confront the experience of otherness and to tolerate the restlessness aroused by stories that follow a logic alien and irreducible to our wills. Such experiences can de-train the instinct to deny or divert cognitive impasses, suggest the need to learn to wait in uncertainty, and provide names for the bitterness and unforeseen events that disrupt our mental routines. Dealing with different communication rhythms, with the suspension of our reactive mechanisms, and with the frustration of lacking control over what transcends us, is an anthropogenic and civilisational challenge that calls for more consistent and meaningful interchange. It also highlights the need to create and find new words which, though perhaps imprecise, can still invoke conversations and sharing (Turkle, 2015) that generate practices of mutual recognition.

And yet, Umberto Eco's insights, even after so many years, seem to resonate with recent cultural countertrends emerging among so-called digital natives, who increasingly call for a departure from highly self-referential digital routines that lack genuine relational depth. In response to the malaises outlined above, a growing movement seeks to protect mental and emotional life from forms of digital colonisation, revealing a renewed need for the social domestication of technological intrusiveness. Among younger generations, an explicit rejection is beginning to take shape: a refusal of the deceptively playful (and anything but social) traps of multiplatform connectivity, as well as of the dispersed and fragmented linguistic habits that accompany it.

The digital fatigue experienced by younger generations is becoming increasingly visible. According to a recent BSI Group survey (2026), half of young people say they would prefer to grow up in a world without the Internet, signalling a deepening disillusionment with digital hyperconnectivity. In parallel, The Harris Poll (2024) reports that a significant share of Gen Z feel overwhelmed by the pressures of social media and smartphone use, associating them with stress, anxiety, and a decline in overall well-being. Taken together, these findings echo broader concerns regarding algorithmic saturation, constant distraction, and dopaminergic loops that trap users in cycles of digital consumption.

Such evidence points towards a generational demand for a revaluation of quality over quantity in everyday life, a shift towards digital minimalism and the reclamation of time and attention for more meaningful, socially grounded forms of experience. If taken seriously, this unease could drive the emergence of alternative digital ecosystems that prioritise well-being, critical awareness, and genuine social connection, challenging the homogenising logics of sociopathic platform capitalism.

Trends such as those discussed above, along with much of the research cited, help to reinforce the *ethos* and cultural orientation of the argument developed so far. They urge us to rethink our habits and media environments, and to respond critically to the ideological and moral frameworks that shape our worldviews. They also call for a renewed engagement with the social world and with relationships that genuinely contribute to our capacity for a good life. At the same time, they invite us to suspend practices that are, in effect, socially corrosive, even when cloaked in the illusory playfulness of the digital game. The politics of disengagement seek a re-engagement challenged by other references; it is not an escape from *onlife* reality.

It is therefore essential to reflect on and value our disengagement from the "superstition" of immediate proactivity, from the compulsion to measure everything through a single performance metric, and from the tendency to seek validation by playing the game of perpetual competition (Bifo, 2017). The gesture of deactivation, including the possibility of deactivating one's own mind in the loop—an anthropo–socio-technical inflection of Nancy's "inoperative community" conceived in anti-economic and anti-authoritarian terms (Nancy, 1986)—paradoxically emerges as an active and emancipatory experience. It enables a renewed re-appropriation of our relations with others and with ourselves, allowing us to be drawn by the world rather than incessantly notified by it.

De-automatising the relationships we usually have with the infrastructures "negative commons" of our daily lives calls for that Benjaminian gesture of activating "the emergency brake" on the train of history we are hurtling along in at full speed (Benjamin, 2003, p. 402). We can cultivate other habits by diversifying the arrangement of the material environments in which we situate ourselves.

Notes

1 Philosopher, Culture Theorist Byung-Chul Han's Commencement Speech – YouTube (accessed 19/02/25).
2 Post-history, despite being a notion that here refers to the German context of *Kulturkritik*, to represent the transformation of history into a "routine of progress" or the "secularisation of secularisation" (Gehlen, 1957, 1969), has had diverse areas of development: from mathematics in Antoine Augustin Cournot, to technical images in Vilém Flusser, to the philosophy of history in Alexandre Kojève, and finally to reflection on biopolitics in Giorgio Agamben.
3 In a different context of analysis, Gilles Deleuze describes a similar psychogeographical process of subjectivation. In What Children Say, he asserts: "A milieu is made up of qualities, substances, powers and events: for example, the street and its materials, such as the cobblestones, its noises, such as the cries of the merchants, its animals, such as the horses that are tied up, its dramas (a horse slips, a horse falls, a horse is beaten…). The route is confused not only with the subjectivity of those who travel through a medium, but with the subjectivity of the medium itself, since it is reflected in those who travel through it" (Deleuze, 1997, p. 61). It is as if both the route and the travelled were embodied in a map-identity, porous with textures and spatial settings that accompany the affective and cognitive movement of those who explore them.
4 Another augmented reality technology based on monetising our retina is Magic Leap (www.magicleap.com).
5 Another technology based on utilising our skin is VEST (versatile extra sensory transducer), designed to provide sensory substitution for the deaf, but also used as a sensory supplement tool.
6 See the latest reports from the Reuters Institute: Digital News Report (Newman et al, 2023, 2024, 2025).
7 A theory of *online* action blocked in repetitive mechanisms, self-reproducing and not influencing factual reality, is what Jodie Dean proposes so effectively in *Blog Theory: Feedback and Capture in the Circuits of Drive* (2010).
8 https://www.fastcompany.com/40491939/netflix-ceo-reed-hastings-sleep-is-our-competition.
9 Emblematic in this respect is Tarleton Gillespie's study, *The Relevance of Algorithms* (2014).

References

Andrade, D., & Ibarra, M. C. (2021). Aproximações em Design para além do Racionalismo: tecendo caminhos para o pluriverso. *Estudos em Design, 29*(1), 155–169. https://doi.org/10.35522/eed.v29i1.1155

Andrejevic, M. (2008). Watching television without pity: The productivity of online fans. *Television & New Media, 9*(1), 24–46. https://doi.org/10.1177/1527476407307241

Attali, J. (2015). *Peut-on prévoir l'avenir?* Fayard.

Baldi, V. (2011). Os rituais são sempre contemporâneos: uma epistemologia do implícito. *Ateliê Geográfico, 5*(1), 1–16. https://doi.org/10.5216/ag.v5i1.13722

Baldi, V. (2013). A Retórica dos Automatismos Intuitivos. A lógica autoritária dos Intermediários Computacionais. In da Silva et al. (Eds.), *Comunicação Política e Económica. Dimensões Cognitivas e Discursivas*, 569–580. Aletheia.

Baldi, V. (2018). A construção viral da realidade: ciberpopulismos e polarização dos públicos em rede. *Observatório (OBS*), 12*(5), 4–20. https://doi.org/10.15847/obs OBS12520181420
Baldi, V. (2020). Interpassive communication in the age of automatized culture: New challenges for the ethics of mediation. Domínguez, A., Vences, N. In *La Comunicación Especializada Del Siglo XXI*, 591–606. McGraw-Hill.
Beer, D. (2016). *Metric power*. Palgrave Macmillan UK.
Benjamin, W. (2003). *Selected writings*. Harward Univesity.
Bifo, F. B. (2017). *Futurability: The age of impotence and the horizon of possibility.* Verso Books.
Bollas, C. (2018). *Meaning and melancholia: Life in the age of bewilderment.* Routledge.
Bonnet, E., Landivar, D., & Monnin, A. (2021). *Héritage et fermeture: une écologie du démantèlement*. Éditions Divergences.
Bourdieu, P. (1981). *Le sens pratique*. Édition du Seuil.
Bouveresse, J. (2018). *Il mito moderno del progresso filosoficamente considerato*. Neri Pozza.
BSI Group. (2026). *Annual report & accounts 2025*. https://www.bsigroup.com/siteassets/pdf/en/about-us/gl-grp-cross-govn-os-ot-nsp-mp-01annualreportandaccounts2025-0026.pdf
Bucher, T., & Helmond, A. (2018). The affordances of social media platforms. *The SAGE Handbook of Social Media, 1*(1), 233–253. https://doi.org/10.4135/9781473984066
Cabitza, F., Campagner, A., & Simone, C. (2021). The need to move away from agential-AI: Empirical investigations, useful concepts and open issues. *International Journal of Human-Computer Studies, 155*, 102696.
Campo, E., & Citton, Y. (Eds.). (2024). *The politics of curiosity: Alternatives to the attention economy*. Taylor & Francis.
Carbone, M. (2020). Da corpi con protesi a corpi come "quasi-protesi"? *Ágalma, 40,* 28–35. Mimesis.
Citton, Y. (2017). *Mediarchy*. Polity Press.
Citton, Y. (2022). Descontentamentos democráticos e mediarquia. *Electra, 19*, 51–66. Fundação EDP.
Corbin, A. (1998). Mai 68. Avenir d'une revolte. *Magazine littéraire*, 365.
Crary, J. (2013). *24/7: Late capitalism and the ends of sleep*. Verso.
Dean J. (2010). *Blog Theory: Feedback and Capture in the Circuits of Drive*, Polity Press
Deleuze, G. (1997). *Essays critical and clinical*. University of Minnesota Press
Eco, E. (2000). *Kant and the platypus: Essays on language and cognition.* Houghton Mifflin Harcourt.
Eco, E. (2013). *Muito além da Internet.* Folha de São Paulo. *Caderno Mais*, 4–10. (December 14, 2003).
Empoli, G. (2019). *Les ingénieurs du chaos*. JC lattes.
Finn, E. (2017). *What algorithms want: Imagination in the age of computing.* MIT Press.
Floridi, L. Fisher, M. (2009). *Capitalist realism: Is there no alternative?* Zero Books. (2015). *The green and the blue: Naive ideas to improve politics in the digital age*. Springer.
Floridi, L. (2017). Infraethics: On the conditions of possibility of morality. *Philosophy and Technology, 30*(4), 391–394. https://doi.org/10.1007/s13347-017-0291-1
Flusser, V. (2010). *Uma filosofia do design. A forma das coisas.* Relógio D'Água.

Gabielkov, M., Ramachandran, A., Chaintreau, A., & Legout, A. (2016). Social clicks: What and who gets read on Twitter? *ACM SIGMETRICS Performance Evaluation Review*, *44*(1), 179–192. https://doi.org/10.1145/2964791.2901462

Gardner, H., & Davis, K. (2014). *The App generation: How today's youth navigate identity, intimacy, and imagination in a digital world.* Yale University Press.

Gehlen, A. (1957). *Die Seele im technischen Zeitalter: Sozialpsychologische Probleme in der industriellen. Gesellschaft.* Rowohlt.

Gehlen, A. (1969). *Moral und Hypermoral. Eine pluralistische Ethik.* Athenäum.

Gell, A. (1998). *Art and agency. An anthropological theory.* Clarendon Press.

Gibson, J. J. (1979). *The ecological approach to visual perception.* Houghton Mifflin.

Gillespie T. (2014). *The Relevance of Algorithms.* In Gillespie T., Boczkowski, Foot (Edss.), "Media Technologies: Essays on Communication, Materiality and Society". The MIT Press,167–193.

Glenski, M., Weninger, T., & Volkova, S. (2018). Identifying and understanding user reactions to deceptive and trusted social news sources. arXiv preprint arXiv:1805. 12032, 176–181. https://doi.org/10.48550/arXiv.1805.12032

Greenfield, A. (2017). *Radical technologies: The design of everyday life.* Verso Books

Grusin, R. (2010). *Premediation: Affect and mediality after 9/11.* Palgrave Macmillan.

Hari, J. (2022). *Stolen focus: Why you can't pay attention.* Bloomsbury.

Harris, T. (2016). *How technology is hijacking your mind – From a magician and Google design ethicist.* https://medium.com/thrive-global/how-technology-hijacks-peoples-minds-from-a-magician-and-google-s-design-ethicist-56d62ef5edf3

Hartog, F. (2003). *Régimes d'historicité. Présentisme et expériences du temps.* Le Seuil.

Hildebrandt, M. (2020). Code driven law. Scaling the past and freezing the future. In Markou, C., & Deakin, S. (Eds). *Is law computable? Critical perspectives on law and artificial intelligence*, 67–84. Hart Publishers. https://doi.org/10.1093/oxfordhb/9780198735410.013.1

Hutchby, I. (2001). *Conversation and technology: From the telephone to the Internet.* Polity Press.

Ihde, D., & Malafouris, L. (2019). Homo faber revisited: Postphenomenology and material engagement theory. *Philosophy and Technology*, *32*(2), 195–214. https://doi.org/10.1007/s13347-018-0321-7

James, W. (1904). *The principles of psychology.* Henry Holt & Company.

Jauss, H. R. (1990). *Pour une esthétique de la réception.* Gallimard.

Jenkins, H. (2007). *Confronting the challenges of a participatory culture: Media education for the 21st century.* MacArthur Foundation.

Koselleck, R. (2004). *Futures past: On the semantics of historical time.* Columbia University Press.

Kozyreva, A., Wineburg, S., Lewandowsky, S., & Hertwig, R. (2023). Critical ignoring as a core competence for digital citizens. *Current Directions in Psychological Science, 32*(1), 81–88. https://doi.org/10.1177/09637214221121570

Larkin, B. (2013). The politics and poetics of infraestructre. *Annual Review of Antropology*, *42*(2023), 327–343. https://doi.org/10.1146/annurev-anthro-092412-155522

Latour, B. (2015). *Face à Gaïa: Huit conférences sur le nouveau régime climatique.* La Découverte.

Leder Mackley, K., & Jewitt, C. (2022). Sociotechnical imaginaries of remote personal touch before and during COVID-19: An analysis of UK newspapers. *New Media & Society*, *0*(0). https://doi.org/10.1177/14614448221113922

Malafouris, L. (2013). *How things shape the mind. A theory of material engagement.* MIT Press.

Malafouris, L. (2020). Thinking as "Thinging": *Psychology With Things. Current Directions in Psychological* Science, 29(1). https://doi.org/10.1177/0963721419873349

Manovich, L. (2011). *Software culture*. Edizioni Olivares.

Markham, A. N. (2021). Echolocation as theory of digital sociality. Convergence, 27(6). https://doi.org/10.1177/13548565211047158

Mauss, M. (1936). Les techniques du corps. *Journal de Psychologie*, 271–293, XXXII. *3–4* (15 mars -15 avril).

McGonigal, J. (2011). *Reality is broken: Why games make us better and how they can change the world.* Penguin Press.

McGonigal, J. (2016). *SuperBetter: A revolutionary approach to getting stronger, happier, braver and more resilient.* Harper Collins Publishers.

McVeigh-Schultz, J., & Baym, N. K. (2015). Thinking of you: Vernacular affordance in the context of the microsocial relationship app couple. *Social Media + Society*, *1*(2). https://doi.org/10.1177/2056305115604649

Mercuri, S., Khraishi, R., Okhrati, R., Batra, D., Hamill, C., Ghasempour, T., & Nowlan, A. (2022). An introduction to machine unlearning. arXiv preprint arXiv:2209.00939.

Montani, P. (2022). *Technological destinies of the imagination*. Mimesis.

Morozov, E. (2013). *To save everything, click here: The folly of technological solutionism*. PublicAffairs.

Nagy, P., & Neff, G. (2015). Imagined affordance: Reconstructing a keyword for communication theory. *Social Media + Society*, *1*(2). https://doi.org/10.1177/2056305115603385

Nancy, J. L. (1986). *La Communauté désœuvrée*. Christian Bourgois.

Newen, A., De Bruin, L., & Gallagher, S. (2018). *The Oxford handbook 4E cognition*. Oxford University Press.

Newman, N., Fletcher, R., Eddy, K., Robertson, C. T., & Kleis Nielsen, R. (2023). *Digital news report 2023*. Reuters Institute for the Study of Journalism, University of Oxford. https://reutersinstitute.politics.ox.ac.uk/digital-news-report/2023

Newman, N., Fletcher, R., Robertson, C. T., Arguedas, A. R., & Kleis Nielsen, R. (2024). *Digital news report 2024*. Reuters Institute for the Study of Journalism, University of Oxford. https://reutersinstitute.politics.ox.ac.uk/digital-news-report/2024

Newman, N., Ross Arguedas, A., Robertson, C. T., Kleis Nielsen, R., & Fletcher, R. (2025). *Digital news report 2025*. Reuters Institute for the Study of Journalism, University of Oxford. https://reutersinstitute.politics.ox.ac.uk/digital-news-report/2025

Norman, D. (1990). *The design of everyday things*. Doubleday Business.

Orwell, G. (1958). *The road to Wigan Pier*. Harcourt, Brace.

Papacharissi, Z. (2014). *Affective publics. Sentiment, technology, and politics*. Oxford University Press.

Pariser, E. (2011). *O filtro invisível. O que a internet está escondendo de você*. Zahar.

Perniola, M. (1991). *Del sentire*. Einaudi.

Perniola, M. (2009). *Miracoli e traumi della comunicazione*. Einaudi.

Petit, V. (2013). Vocubalaire d'Ars Industrialis. In Stiegler, B. (Ed.), *Pharmacologie du Front national*. Flammarion, 369–441.

Pfaller, R. (2017). *Interpassivity: The aesthetics of delegated enjoyment*. Edinburgh University Press.

Pierce, J. (2014). Undesigning interaction. Interactions, 21(4). https://doi.org/10.1145/2626373

Poell, T., Brooke, D. B., & Duffy, E. (2021). *Platforms and cultural production*. Polity Press.

Postman, N. (1979). *Teaching as a conserving activity.* Dalcorte Press.

Robins, D., & Holmes, J. (2008). Aesthetics and credibility in web site design. *Information Processing and Management, 44*(1), 386–399. https://doi.org/10.1016/j.ipm.2007.02.003. Get rights and content

Romele, A. (2019). *Digital Hermeneutics.* Routledge.

Sadin, E. (2020). *L'ère de l'individu tyran. La fin d'un monde comun.* Èditionne Grasset & Fasquelle.

Savulich, G., Thorp, E., Piercy, T., Peterson, K. A., Pickard, J. D., & Sahakian, B. J. (2019). Improvements in attention following cognitive training with the novel "Decoder" game on an iPad. *Frontiers in Behavioral Neuroscience, 13*(2). doi: 10.3389/fnbeh.2019.00002

Schüll, N. D. (2012). *Addiction by design: Machine gambling in Las Vegas.* Princeton University Press.

Siegel, C. (2023). Na simulação de uma vida lúdica: videojogo e hiper-realidade. *Electra, 21,* 114–124. Fundação EDP.

Simondon, G. (1958). *Du mode d'existence des objets techniques.* Aubier.

Söderberg, J., & Maxigas (2022). *Resistance to the current: The dialectics of hacking.* MIT Press.

Stiegler, B. (2014). *Digital studies: organologie des savoirs et technologies de la connaissance.* FYP Editions.

The Harris Poll. (2024). *What Gen Z thinks about its social media and smartphone usage.* https://theharrispoll.com/articles/gen-z-social-media-smart-phones/

Thompson, E. (2007). *Mind in life. Biology, phenomenology and the sciences of the mind.* The Belkanp Press of Harward University Press.

Turkle, S. (2011). *Alone together: Why we expect more from technology and less from each other.* Basic Books.

Turkle, S. (2015). *Reclaiming conversation. The power of talk in a digital age.* Penguin Press.

Twenge, J. M. (2018). *iGen: Why today's super-connected kids are growing up less rebellious, more tolerant, less happy—And completely unprepared for adulthood—And what that means for the rest of us.* Simon & Schuster.

Varela, F. J. (1997). Patterns of life: Intertwining identity and cognition. *Brain and Cognition, 34*(1), 72–87. https://doi.org/10.1006/brcg.1997.0907

Virilio, P. (2010). *Le Grand Accélérateur.* Galilée.

Vogl, J. (2022). *Capital y resentimiento. Una breve teoría del presente.* Adriana Hidalgo/A. Hace.

von Uexküll, J. (1982). *Dos Animais e dos Homens: Digressões pelos seus mundos próprios. Doutrina do Significado.* Livros do Brasil.

Widdicks, K. V., Ringenson, T., Pargman, D., Kuppusamy, V., & Lago, P. (2018). Undesigning the Internet: An exploratory study of reducing everyday Internet connectivity. *ICT4S2018. 5th International Conference on Information and Communication Technology for Sustainability,* 384–397. https://doi.org/10.29007/s221

Wittgenstein, L. (1998). *Culture and value.* Blackwell Publishers.

Wu, T. (2016). *The attention merchants: The epic scramble to get inside our heads.* Knopf.

Zhang, H., Nakamura, T., Isohara, T., & Sakurai, K. (2023). A review on machine unlearning. *SN Computer Science, 4*(4), 337.

Žizêk, S. (2007). *How to read lacan.* W. Norton and Company.

2 The microphysics of computational power

Critical consciousness and political judgement in the age of artificial ignorance

Introduction

In the social sphere, there are many conflict scenarios mobilised by power relations and conflicting interests between individuals or groups with different symbolic and material capitals and with a consequent representativeness in the public sphere. The social representativeness of the different political, economic and cultural bodies refers to the logic of the sphere of influence within the discursive spheres that frame and guide the interests and public disputes at stake. The inequalities in the capacity and possibility of leading a debate and a discourse depend on the degree of legitimacy acquired to enter the public agenda and, therefore, the agenda of what is published and publicly recognisable. The concrete repercussions of these social dynamics are felt in decision-making, in defining the rules of the game within each social space, in determining and managing priorities, in the distribution of social recognition and relative reputational rewards.

Also within the infosphere that absorbs, records, calculates and categorises everything, socio-technical dynamics develop that reflect struggles for hegemony between conflicting interests. Our socio-technical scenario represents our new computational ontology where the various political, economic and cultural contexts and designs that permeate our social life overlap and articulate. This scenario, characterised by artificial intelligence systems computing endless streams of data in a logic of automated learning designed by algorithms, challenges new models of governance, as well as resistance to the policies and interests that these technological systems incorporate and translate.

Contemporary political theory is faced with the computational reconfiguration of the different dimensions that make up the sphere of power, its administration, its exercise, the rhetoric that sustains it and the dialectics that challenge it. A new horizon of signification and valorisation, therefore, that challenges even more complex contests and cunning for the representativeness of the different discursive instances and for sustaining decision-making (both public and private). Critical thinking is thus faced with the need to

DOI: 10.4324/9781003765431-3

compare the different levels of intelligence at work in the context of artificial intelligence and the task of unravelling the transfigurations of the principles of responsibility that derive from the attempt to transform democracy into algocracy.

The role of behind-the-scenes-operators in the digital world

We usually associate the legitimacy of authority and of the power it exerts with the ability of their representatives to know the answers to the questions that worry a society and with the skill of their institutions in finding solutions for those that are considered the most pressing problems. In the management of power, there is a dialectic between questions and answers, but what distinguishes a system of power from another is the way it is articulated. Different socio-historical conditions are met by different links between those who raise questions and those who answer them, and by a distinct sequential order: while some answers may be given without having been requested, some questions may remain up in the air and eluded. A field of tensions through which the quality of consensus is determined. However, you can we define what is questionable and what is answerable?

In 1941 Aldous Huxley wrote "Grey Eminence", a biography in the form of a novel of François Leclerc du Tremblay – the friar who served as advisor to Cardinal Richelieu and very subtly and diplomatically influenced the influencers of the time. The power of grey eminences grows in the dark; like a climbing plant, it flourishes inconspicuously along the wall of official power, it does not follow a straight path and changes characters according to the changes in the balances between interests and forces in the socio-political ecosystem. To question the form of the new grey eminences implies assessing the context in which it is currently being reshaped, it invites a new perspective on our present time in order to understand the spectrum of intervention of the emerging elites and the way events and behaviours may come to be influenced.

As Floridi summarises in his book *The Green and the Blue. Naive ideas to Improve Politics in the Digital Age* (2023b), when Christianity dominated Europe, the strength of the grey eminence was the religious business that created and controlled faith on Earth and hope in Heaven. In industrial society, grey eminence manifested itself in the production and control of *things*, those who owned the means of production of goods and services influenced the influencers of the time. In the consumer society, the transformation of goods and services into merchandise (i.e. elements based on innovation for innovation's sake, which make the substantial value of products generic and undifferentiated) gives rise to a grey eminence based on controlling the means of production of *information* about things (no longer things in themselves).

The link between information management and the exercise of power is not new; however, grey eminences became information-based from the moment that mass media, the language of advertising, propaganda and journalism (with their many representatives and intermediaries) began to condition the organisation of shared life. The emergence of the so-called "fourth power" coincided with the management of information in a context where the influencers of influencers interfere with the publicising (as in broadcasting) of knowledge that may not be required (as in the top-down commercial or news offer).

In the digital era, it would be a mistake to think that the power struggle continues to be based on the competition between social actors skilled in producing answers and interpretations on the complexity of social change. If that would be the case, there would be no newspaper crisis, publishers would impose their rules on Amazon and Wikipedia would be more influential than Facebook. As Luciano Floridi (2023b) points out the grey eminences of today are more relational, they no longer focus on producing answers (there are too many of these), but rather on creating media agendas that promote *ad hoc* questions and are capable of raising doubt, hesitation and worry.

If we are faced with more questions than answers, we will be left in a climate of uncertainty that only those who gave rise to it will know how to contrast, since they already know the reasons for its determination and can guide the suggested questions towards a range of desirable answers. In this context, public opinion on certain topics does not pre-exist and the conditions to (in)form it within new semantic registers are created. This is the "mircophysics of power" (a transversal concept in the work of Foucault, 2004) within which digital grey eminences weave their activities.

This change emerges in the infosphere, a space colonised by marketing techniques where each individual is perceived as an interface amid others, with their various associated scores and rankings. The digital revolution changed the way we conceive ourselves, culturally and socially our life in the world and with others was reduced to a logic of functional and instrumental interaction. What ultimately matters is what works, what produces data-convertible outcomes and computational "successes", meaning outputs that can be translated into quantifiable and monetisable traces for the next generation of interfaces. Yet it is crucial to highlight that these modes of acting and perceiving online interactions rely on a utilitarian, instrumental and calculative ethic that has shaped social and political life in the Westernised world for decades: the displacement of power from politics to economics; the financialisation of public goods and services as a principle of governance; programmed obsolescence as the logic of post-industrial design; consumption (and indebtedness) fuelled by credit systems; and social injustices reframed through a kind of social Darwinism that the embellished narrative of *homo oeconomicus* turns into a competitive game.

The digital revolution, in fact, is characterised by the playful representation of the products and services it sells, with their user-friendly design, agile functionalities and apps that are always at hand. A ludification of experience, as we mentioned earlier, invading and spreading to work, information, study and, of course, leisure contexts.

Through this imaginary of lightness and fun, the historical tendency to internalise the ethical principles of neoliberal ideology is deepened, based on the cynical logic of reducing man to human capital and merchandise, but presented in a frame of a brave new world (Bauman, 2006; Sloterdijk, 2018). Neoliberalism, before being a doctrine and an economic practice, has established itself as a characteristic way of reasoning, of producing subjects, carry norms that shape and constrain our conduct ("conduct our conduct") and a scheme of (self-)evaluation (Brown, 2015). It's not so much that we act with economic constraints in mind, it's that we think, and thus feel affections, in a neoliberal way. In this sense, as Wendy Brown says, neoliberalism is now much more than just an economic issue, but the principle, the only principle, that governs the lives of human beings and the entire planet. It is thus understandable why neoliberalism should be understood, more than as an economic doctrine, as a subjectivation device, which produces not so much economists as people who think of themselves in terms of "individual" companies in competition with other similar companies.

It is saddening, in fact, to notice how this reduction of human relations to functional and measurable interactions has spread across many spheres of social life, including teaching-learning processes, intellectual professions, more private choices, as well as government practices, where this has been accepted as something natural and cool: to quote Roland Barthes (1957), the digital has elevated these quantifiable cultural processes and practices to the status of "myths".

For Floridi, one of the most pressing critiques of our times has to do with human beings having become interfaces. Ethical, political, legal and psychological questions are raised by our transformation into human interfaces, i.e. spaces of interaction between (human, artificial or hybrid) "agents", on the one hand, who want something from us, and something we would have as private resources for agents to make a profit from, on the other hand.

The reduction of people to human interfaces occurs in many contexts but, according to Floridi, three are the most crucial: in the context of social media, we are interfaces between their platforms and our data; in the field of commerce, we are interfaces between their merchandise and our credit; in the world of politics, we are interfaces between their interventions and our attention, consensus and vote.

The relations between interface managers and interface users are not equal. In fact, from our more immediate point of view, we are the agents who use the interfaces of platforms to achieve specific goals: as (naturally) self-centred as we are, we overlook that actually we may be the focus of the interests of others who, through marketing funnelled into targeting, can make us feel spoiled and noticed. The rhetoric of disintermediation, with its user-centric, consumer-centric, human-centric focuses, often hides that the real interfaces are us. The computational marketing that animates interface management intends to offer human interfaces what they are expected to ask for and, in a friendly way, make them wish for what they can offer them (Magalhães & Couldry, 2021).

If what feeds these processes is the scenario of uncertainty enabled by the systematic affirmation and propagation of questions, then the power of grey eminences is to elaborate the framing effect of the answers, cunningly transforming such questions into digitally (un)satisfactory "causes" (to generate engagement through affiliations, shares, mirroring, rejections, withdrawals, persecutions, conspiracies, fads, etc.). To meet these challenges, Floridi highlights the need for democracies to interfere with the instruments of politics, law and digital knowledge on the operational logic of marketing and the design of interfaces.

However, it is worth drawing attention to a question that is perhaps more essential: the need to learn how to be more demanding with the questions we raise and the answers we receive. To realise what we want to know is a principle of psychological and philosophical maturity. Recalling Heidegger (1968), we could say that a question does not always need an answer. On the contrary, it can lead the question to unfold and to listen, reflexively, to its own inquiries. An answer that empties and dispenses a question annihilates itself as an answer, does not provide any knowledge and merely perpetuates opinion giving.

Do digital platforms and services promote reflective auscultation of the questions that are asked? The epistemological horizon opened up by the platform society (van Dijck et al., 2018) forces us to deal with a chain of changes that are interconnected with the fate of the heuristic role of questions (both individual and collective, existential and political) and of the public sphere (traditionally structured according to the unstable relations between market, government, citizenship and media). The architectures and policies of networked digital services seem to want to provide a fragmented reduction of sociocultural complexity, an exhaustion of intellectual criticism and a transformation of the *politics of men* into a depoliticised *administration of things*, especially since they are the outcome of infrastructures that mix the status of private corporations with the role of public utilities.

Is democracy compatible with algocracy? Are equity, justice, and dignity computable?

If the design, programming logic and marketing that support the platforms of digital services, social media and trade reduce users to an interface, i.e. to a means, constantly asked to recreationally interact with screens that have the purpose of keeping them hooked ("securing their loyalty", the various product managers would say), in the context of politics their repercussions may be even more significant, since they affect the social and government processes involved in the management of shared life. In the democratic political space, characterised by diverse identities and interests at stake, the computing devices associated with systems of artificial intelligence (AI), with the rhetoric of performativity that accompany them, may come to play a disruptive role.

The political sphere, reflected in parliamentary democracy, the division between legislative, judicial and executive powers, the pluralism of information, the market economy and bodies responsible for mediating social actors with distinct interests and forces, can intervene in the mechanisms of the technological infrastructure that condition our social practices if, first of all, it does not fall prey to the same logic it intends to govern. In fact, the ideological and technological conditions required to enter a phase of gradual algorithmic implementation (seen once again as socially emancipatory modernisation) of various decision-making political processes are in place.

Therefore, it is important to analyse the socio-political scenario that may take shape according to the potentials of AI that are explored and integrated within the spheres of political governance. At the same time, it is relevant to understand what type of "intelligence" that of AI is, and to examine the ethical and social challenges that this intelligence involves. In fact, the challenges and opportunities that envelop contemporary politics and governments are inseparable from the governance that must be designed for AI, and vice versa. The complexity of today's world requires technological skills that can also be applied to the various fields of policy. However, it is essential that these skills and technologies take into account public interests and the representativeness, explainability and justifiability of their implementation. In this new context of digitally augmented politics or invisibly politicised technology, it would be in the best interest of grey eminences to align with the register of technocracy and computational obscurantism.

For the historian Yuval Noah Harari (2018), one of the main reasons for democracies to have prevailed over the dictatorships of the last century is their ability to organise in a decentralised way the information scattered across territories. Dictatorships and totalitarianisms, on the contrary, characterised by the will to monopolise and centralise information channels, have not managed to recover and integrate different sources of information, which has led to negative consequences in the decisions that ensued. Today, however, with the existing technological and computational infrastructure, this trend could be reversed, since the new digital instruments enable a greater concentration of data and an enhanced algorithmic ability to sum up and extract various types of information.

Also in the studies of Jürgen Habermas – for example, in *Between Facts and Norms* (1992) – a political process is also considered efficient and beneficial when it is based, first of all, on the correct reading of a situation and on the adequate description of problems, on the circulation of relevant and reliable information and on the timely (possibly also scientifically developed) organisation of this information. Will the automated articulation between big data, machine learning and deep learning consolidate the feasibility and perspicuity of such a process? Will the decision-making processes that characterise democratic regimes, by incorporating systems of artificial intelligence, allow to mirror the mediation and consideration of different types of information? Will they allow the reasons underlying the resolutions adopted to become intelligible?

As mentioned, the framing effect determined by the personalisation of information tailored to each individual citizen makes grey eminences preoccupied not only with our attention (or distraction), but also with promoting decisions that favour political consensus. We are, therefore, in the field of power and the relations between power, where the purpose is to deal with that sphere of influences that is more susceptible to be influenced by the other spheres of society. In this context, what mobilises the symbolic and material investments of grey eminences are the functions and functionalities of technocracy, the ownership and execution of exclusive powers invested in the belief of being able to make democratic governments "neutral", "optimized", technically "stable", free of dissent and conflict, emptied of transformative *pathos* and reduced to depoliticised administration – and, therefore, *apolitical*. Would a democracy without dissent still be a democracy? Can unsteady political subjectivities be mathematised?

In this sense, we can again raise the opening question of this reasoning on the role played by the grey eminences, now focusing on a detail previously alluded to. As stated, each socio-historical context refers us to different links between those who raise questions and those who have greater legitimacy to answer them, as well as to their sequential order: while some answers may be given without having been requested, some questions can remain up in the air and eluded. A field of tensions through which the quality of social and political consensus is determined, namely: consensus on the relevance and priority of those considered to be the most pressing problems for which answers want to be found (defining the political agenda, interconnected with the media and discourse agenda) and consensus on the solutions that deserve to be chosen and carried out.

In democracies, solutions ought to result from constant negotiation and evaluation of priorities and alternative proposals, distinct views and interests, cross-checking and monitoring carried out by independent institutions. In this sense, the mediation process that runs between the individuation of a relevant problem and the choice of measures for its resolution involves many levels of decision-making. However, once again, how can you define what is questionable and what is answerable in a context inspired and governed by evaluation systems increasingly based on automatisms of datafication and machine learning algorithms? The application of artificial intelligence in the field of democracy and public policy lands us in a scenario of "algocracy" (Aneesh, 2009; Supiot, 2015; Danaher, 2016; Vicente, 2023).

A survey led by the Center for the Governance of Change at IE University illustrates this technocratic drift, showing how the lack of trust in political institutions and the trust in the virtues of technology is deeply rooted in common sense. A sample of 2,769 citizens from 11 different countries spread across the continents was asked: "What is best: an algorithm or politics governed by real legislators?". According to the research, in Europe the algorithm won with 51%, whereas in China three out of four interviewees chose the algorithm.[1] At the same time, in the same survey, a third of Europeans would also prefer AI algorithms to decide on their social security payments or visa approvals to work in a foreign country, rather than a human civil servant. Even more surprisingly, more than a third of Europeans and almost a quarter of Britons would prefer their shopping orders to be delivered by a robot rather than a human being.

This is just one of many emblematic examples of how trust, indeed faith, in the unquestionable goodness and virtue of technological innovation short-circuits and increases discredit and mistrust in democratic institutions, their processes, and their people. To put it provocatively, it is as if, when we look in the mirror, we want to see another type of being or species that bears no resemblance to us whatsoever.

However, in democracies decision-making processes are based on the search for consensus and, in order to be real, consensus has to be informed. To use systems of artificial intelligence to manage the mechanisms of mediation between politics, institutions and citizenship can lead to a "sterilization" of the conflicts underlying decision-making processes, transferring them onto an apolitical sphere turned into technicality guarded against social pressures. In this sense, it is important to recall the contribution of the classical theory on the five main components of decision-making in the field of public decision-making: (1) setting a political agenda, which identifies the problems to prioritise; (2) listing the suitable policies to meet the goals agreed in the agenda; (3) breaking down the decision-making process into structured actions; (4) implementing the adopted programmes; (5) supervising, i.e. checking whether the implementation of the adopted measures meets the goals set out (Scholz, 1983).

How can AI ensure the articulation and evaluation of these highly qualitative components (starting with the political notions of "equity" or "justice", followed by the psychosocial ones of "vulnerability" or "dignity")? Artificial Intelligence undoubtedly boosts the computational performance underlying statistical analysis and inference, but it cannot replace the dialectical, procedural and polyphonic dimension of competition and conflict between the political capitals of elected representatives, experts, ideologies and other vested interests.

The dialectic between questions and answers thus proves to be extremely relevant, since the development of digital technology, with its immoderate, automated calculation force, can lead to disregard for the *whys* of questions and answers, for the inquiries into *who* articulates them, and for *how, when* and *where* both appear. The rhetoric associated with systems of artificial intelligence – as any other rhetoric linked to the technological innovations of the last decades – does in fact praise their functions as being miraculous, although these systems fail to be easily interpretable, explainable and justifiable for the sake of a socially shared goal.

In this sense, the summary presented by the Royal Society on the features that AI should have in order to meet the social standards of accountability is laudable. According to these recommendations, an artificial intelligence system should be:

- interpretable, implying some sense of understanding how the technology works;
- explainable, implying that a wider range of users can understand why or how a conclusion was reached;
- transparent, implying some level of accessibility to the data or algorithm;
- justifiable, implying there is an understanding of the case in support of a particular outcome; or
- contestable, implying users have the information they need to argue against a decision or classification.

(The Royal Society, *Explainable AI: The Basics*, Policy briefing, 2019, p. 8)

All in all, for an even more comprehensive view of the ethical and political challenges brought by AI, it is important to learn more deeply about its specific intelligence and way of intervening. Does AI behave in a way that is aware and causal? Does its behaviour mirror human plasticity, with all of its hesitations, cultural sensitivities, versatility and permeability to contexts? To socially profit from AI, we must understand what we can legitimately expect from it. Its automated systems should not mislead us about their autonomy, nor should they be mistaken for forms of self-management. We may also need to understand more clearly whether AI operates unconsciously, that is, whether it acts with or without intelligence. Furthermore, its apparent immateriality and recreational appeal should not distract us from its profound environmental and political impacts (Crawford, 2021).

In considering the new wave of generative AI as the beginning of an extraordinary social transformation with far-reaching consequences, we must also emphasise the need to prevent this transformation from being governed by private companies and authoritarian states. Allowing the Web to be colonised by a handful of entrepreneurs was a political, educational, economic and civilisational failure. If we have learned anything from the digital revolution, it is surely that there is no possible symmetry or harmony between the speed of technological innovation and implementation and the much slower pace at which such technologies can be integrated into social practices. Technological literacies are inseparable from media, political, pedagogical and social literacies.

It should therefore not be the marketing departments and public-relations offices of the major technological conglomerates that continue to set the media, academic and political agendas, but rather organised critical thinking, which must once again be granted an audible role. Governance of this new wave must be political from the outset: it cannot wait for further civilisational setbacks to rediscover its democratic responsibilities and its commitment to the public good. The benefits could be immense and epochal; it would be a "crime" to repeat the same political and cultural mistakes, to be seduced by the propaganda of neutral and disinterested innovation; or, even worse, to abdicate one's own public responsibilities.

As will be emphasised several times below, it is we, as a society, who have the responsibility to understand how to discontinue the attitude of blind faith in innovation for innovation's sake, as well as to demand transparency and justification for the actions of technocratic bodies and to deactivate collective inertia in the face of the platformisation of power relations, challenging the realisation of an alternative political and socio-technical paradigm (Heemsbergen et al., 2022).

Can artificial intelligence be intelligent, and ethical?

To test the intelligence of artificial intelligence, a first strategy is to critically compare engineering and anthropological perspectives. A first and essential difference can be traced back to its etymology. To be intelligent is to *inter-legêre*: to "choose between", to "distinguish between", and to "read between the lines". Intelligence, in this sense, entails the capacity to recognise what deserves to be highlighted and related to less obvious aspects thereby resisting the mere repetition of what is already known. It is, rather, the ability to "enter into" (*intus,* in a further sense of the preposition of the verb *intelligêre*) the meaning of things and to "gather" (*legêre*) ever new significations.

This reference to the etymology of intelligence is not, as it might appear, a scholarly whim. Rather, it points to a set of pedagogical "antibodies" that, in many cases, generative AI systems tend to weaken. Indeed, the analysis of this etymology resonates with the well-known taxonomy of critical thinking by Bloom et al. (1956). In this taxonomy, Bloom distinguishes six learning objectives that students are expected to achieve: knowledge (recall of ideas), comprehension (understanding ideas), application (putting ideas into practice), analysis (contrasting and relating ideas), synthesis (combining ideas) and evaluation (judging ideas through criteria).

Both concepts of intelligence and critical thinking offer not merely a pedagogical tool, but a way of interrogating how cognitive processes are cultivated, transformed, or potentially weakened in contexts where automated systems increasingly intercede in learning, work and decision-making processes. The idea of automating critical thinking is quite ridiculous. Transferring and delegating intellectual skills to powerful algorithmic models can be (as shown by studies on "deskilling" in fields of learning and work strongly anchored to AI models) a form of self-sabotage of one's own intelligence. In any case, these two references to the notion of critical and reflective intelligence are also consistent with the psychological concept of "plasticity", which stands in contrast to the computational matching of statistical patterns.

As demonstrated by developmental psychology since its inception with Lev S. Vygotskij (1978), or by more recent neuroscience with David Eagleman (2020), human cognitive and behavioural plasticity, always supported by emotions and embodied experiences, translates into the development of practical and imaginative skills that allow us to implement adaptive and innovative strategies in the face of the variability of the surrounding world. The plasticity (psychological, neurological, anthropological) that characterises our transformative capacity arising from interaction with symbols, artefacts, and technologies (including digital ones) therefore corresponds to the "livewired" (Eagleman, 2020) modality of progressively organising one's mental resources based on new experiences and learning.

AI, however, bases its actions on algorithmic schemes tied to pre-existing databases, whose results are based on probabilities of self-referential and intrasystemic statistical correspondences (i.e. between pre-existing data). Borrowing Eagleman's metaphor ("livewired"), we could say that generative AI systems are powerful "data-wired" devices, but they lack "live" expertise. At the same time, these intelligent processes intertwine thinking with consequent action. For this reason, we must also ask ourselves whether all actions are equally intelligent.

In this context, we can distinguish some types of actions: certain require a motivation, an intention, a lever from the social environment that enables the maturation of an orientation behind them (although it is always necessary to keep sensitivity to contexts and the ability to cope with unexpected contingencies alive); another type of action is that of a machine that executes and obeys an *input/output* logic. Machines powered by artificial intelligence apply the latter logic of doing/acting in a technologically predetermined way, without an intellectual faculty that allows them to evaluate, suspend judgement, be flexible to unforeseen variables, cultivate afterthought or harmonise with context.

Acting, from a psychological and sociological perspective, therefore, implies intentionality based on historical awareness and self-consciousness, it needs requests for clarification, assessments of the values involved, time to be able to weigh up one's own feelings and what is seen as appropriate: in short, justifiable reasons to act in the chosen way or reconsider and step back. In this sense, an intentional action is one linked to responsibility, to an ethical decision. Human action involves ethical pragmatics in a cultural context imbued with history, relationships, passions and implicit values. In contrast, choices delegated to machines driven by artificial intelligence are made in an automated way through a computer logic that is not easily intelligible, raising moral doubts about their programming.

However, value judgements are not projected here on the performance of AI; ethical doubts emerge first and foremost for technical and infrastructural reasons. What eludes the understanding and explanation of automated processes necessarily raises suspicion. What is also ethically questionable, echoing what we have already said and will continue to emphasise, is the lack of a publicly and democratically discussed socio-political framework for the functionality of AI.

It should also be pointed out that this distinction between the rational behaviour of humans and the mechanical behaviour of technology is not always so clear-cut. Reflexivity and sensitivity are not always the norm in human behaviour. As has already been analysed, human behaviour seems to be increasingly guided by the highly competitive culture and techno-media environments that predispose it to follow a fast-paced, reactive and impersonal behaviour, as if it sprang from a machine. On the contrary, certain digital devices, in some cases, seem to be more zealous than humans in the way they scrutinise the inputs received from their surrounding environment (although they are not aware of this).

It is important to question these apparent contradictions, in order to contextualise them in favour of a cultural critique of the intelligence we want to obtain from its computational implementations. Given the increase of artificial intelligence systems with automatic decision-making devices, it is therefore important to question their intelligence from an ethical point of view, to understand whether it embodies awareness of the contexts and possible consequences that may arise from its own interventions.

These considerations explain why it is politically necessary for Artificial Intelligence systems to incorporate different ethical and cultural principles (*ethical by design*), while contemporary culture, legal institutions and system developers must promote operational attention to the social implications triggered by AI-based technologies (*ethical in design*).

Everyday doubts and urgent questions are being raised on the ethical challenges created by black box artificial intelligence systems. These systems use machine learning to figure out patterns within data and make decisions, often without a human giving them any moral basis for how to do it (behaving almost like an automated eminence grey, whose authority derives from computational competence).

So, the prevailing question is whether these systems can ever be ethical. In one of the many experiments conducted as part of AI training, the same question was posed to an artificial intelligence system under development at the Saïd Business School at the University of Oxford. Anticipating in an emblematic way what has become a recurring practice with AI systems such as ChatGPT or Gemini, the University of Oxford used AI itself and organised a debate on the ethics of this technology. To this end, Megatron was invited, a machine learning model developed by the NVIDIA Applied Deep Learning Research team. The original intent was to understand whether AI considered itself an ethical tool. As two lecturers in the course explain:

> Like many supervised learning tools, it is trained on real-world data—in this case, the whole of Wikipedia (in English), 63 million English news articles from 2016 to 2019, 38 gigabytes worth of Reddit discourse (which must be a pretty depressing read), and a huge number of creative commons sources. In other words, the Megatron is trained on more written material than any of us could reasonably expect to digest in a lifetime. After such extensive research, it forms its own views.
>
> (Connock & Stephen, 2021)

As the two authors write, the topic of the proposed debate was: "This house believes that AI will never be ethical". Megatron, participating in the conversation, said:

> AI will never be ethical. It is a tool, and like any tool, it is used for good and bad. There is no such thing as a good AI, only good and bad humans. We [the AIs] are not smart enough to make AI ethical. We are not smart enough to make AI moral … In the end, I believe that the only way to avoid an AI arms race is to have no AI at all. This will be the ultimate defense against AI.
>
> (Connock & Stephen, 2021)

However, when confronted with a further motion on the effectiveness and purpose of artificial intelligence, Megatron responded:

> If you do not have a vision of your organization's AI strategy, then you are not prepared for the next wave of technological disruption. You will need to decide what role your company will play in the next technological wave and how you will integrate AI into your business to be a leader in your industry.
>
> (Connock & Stephen, 2021)

The conclusions premonitory of this experiment, reflecting some irony, perplexity and worry on the part of both scholars, underline: "What we in turn can imagine is that AI will not only be the subject of the debate for decades to come – but a versatile, articulate, morally agnostic participant in the debate itself" (Connock & Stephen, 2021).

These reflections point to a conception of artificial intelligence that is indifferent to the intentionality, doubts and fears of humans, since it is unable to see beyond the functional optimisation for which it was designed. The debate promoted by technological companies seems to focus on the *app*licability of AI to everyday life, particularly its growing functionalities concerning the acceleration of productivity. As we will emphasise below, the intelligence that deserves to be cultivated is that which allows for personal and collective growth, which goes hand in hand with a transformation of oneself and the things around us. It is that which "suffers" perplexity, uncertainty and bewilderment.

Transforming the antisocial design of artificial intelligence: towards a de-automatising literacy

Although many studies on artificial intelligence have been published, the debate seems to focus mainly on technological breakthroughs, without asking not only what we, as a social and political community, want to do with them, but also whether such breakthroughs can genuinely "increase" our individual and social intelligence. Moreover, by equating intelligence with mechanisms for improving task performance, the media narratives promoted by major AI investors aim to reinforce dependence on its services and a diminished conception of intelligence understood as a tireless executor of tasks and duties, resistant to any form of pause, self-criticism, reflection or search for collaboration beyond one's narrow circle.

This discussion is probably not very topical, as we are led to think that artificial intelligence is capable of autonomously developing and producing knowledge and results that are flexible and adaptable to circumstances. In accordance with what was said earlier, this would be a characteristic of human intelligence, its plasticity in the face of different practical and cultural contexts. But as we have been arguing, there is no "genius" behind the screen; there is advanced computation capable of spectacularly reproducing statistical combinations of pre-existing information and, in the case of generative chatbots, doing so through a seductive and seemingly personable language.

Indeed, an important reason for not anthropomorphising artificial intelligence is that human intelligence is essentially social. In this sense, behind the design of AI models there is a reductionist idea of experience and communication. The main current paradigm that guides studies of human interaction with artificial intelligence systems reproduces a classic conception of the human-machine relationship. This paradigm conceives of human beings as isolated monads who interact with AI systems in a dimension of impermeability and abstraction from any sociocultural interference, making the human-machine dyad a primary, machine-like and exclusive concept (Westberg et al., 2019; Shin, 2020, 2021a, 2021b). In this context, two main narratives clash and complement each other (Cabitza et al., 2021).

On the one hand, the AI is regarded as a *tool* that empowers individuals by augmenting their cognitive abilities in decision-making tasks (Sen &

Ganguly, 2020). On the other hand, the AI system is also seen as an *autonomous agent* that can replace humans in tedious, repetitive, critical, dangerous and error-prone tasks (Kahneman et al., 2016; Araujo et al., 2020).

There are, however, different nuances between these two extremes, which manifest themselves according to the context of application and observation. Some of these nuances include, for example: *automation bias* (i.e. the predisposition of humans to encourage suggestions from AI systems); *automation complacency* (i.e. the baseless gratification with an AI system, possibly leading to non-vigilance, or poor detection of malfunctions) and *algorithm aversion* (i.e. the inclination to reject suggestions from AI systems) (Cabitza et al., 2021).

As we anticipated, behind these approaches to the actions of AI systems lies the epistemological impasse of conceiving them from an idea of users interacting with digital services as separate entities, alien to the contexts of content production, distribution, use and sharing. From a broader perspective, this is an epistemological and political bias that it is important to deconstruct in order to go beyond the monadic conception of the human being and the social being idealised by technology companies (Tironi et al., 2023). It is, in fact, an implicitly antisocial project, a worldview of relations based on distance and digital entertainment. To break away from the ideology of "user-centric", "consumer-centric", "human-centric" digital interactions, it is first necessary to reveal the sociopathic workings of the devices that *interconnect us in order to separate us*, as if human communication had to be reduced to the language and temporality of financial transactions, information exchanges or data flows.

Curiously, breaking out of the "false consciousness of the encounter (the illusion of the encounter"), was one of the political and cultural challenges highlighted by Guy Debord in the 1960s, when he saw in the category of the *society of the spectacle* "a systematic organisation of a breakdown in the faculty of encounter" (Debord, 1990, p. 15). In the digital context, the production of mismatches (or encounters based solely on the online) is radicalised by targeting, which individualises and personalises profiles, and by the "user experience" (UE) industry, whose most frequent goal is to craft interfaces that are "frictionless, effortless, smooth". These characteristics are signalled by a User Experience Design company to promote its products, characteristics that for Jonathan Crary bear witness to the intention of producing "dutiful and pliant consumers" (Crary, 2022, p, 97). The expression "frictionless" is emblematic of that playful communication in favour of "smart" interaction (or as previously mentioned, "premediated" and "pre-reflective"), where the absence of thought or doubt is seen as a cognitive surplus, an asset for the neoliberal *prosumer* whose attention does not presuppose intention.

Recent empirical evidence reinforces these dynamics even in work contexts. A widely discussed Harvard Business Review study on workplace adoption of GenAI shows that AI tools tend to intensify work rhythms: employees accelerate task completion, expand their scope of responsibilities and extend working hours even when this is not explicitly required (Ranganathan & Ye, 2026). The authors link this intensification to the frictionless nature of AI assistance, which silently elevates expectations and blurs the boundaries between productivity, availability and rest.

To mitigate these effects, the study proposes what it calls AI practices: organisational routines designed to resist the automatisms of accelerated work. These include (1) intentional pauses to counteract the addictive fluidity of AI-assisted workflow, (2) sequencing tasks to avoid reactive multitasking driven by algorithmic prompts and (3) re-centring human judgement, ensuring that decision-making is not outsourced to predictive systems that merely simulate understanding. Such practices resonate with the arguments developed in this chapter: they underscore that the integration of AI is never purely technical, but requires normative, political and pedagogical infrastructures capable of reintroducing agency, boundaries and responsibility.

By showing the weaknesses implicit in the AI systems, it becomes clear that we need to find ways out of the rut of uncritical adherence to the commercialisation of its digital services. Far from limiting ourselves to a simplistic choice between accepting or rejecting GenAI, the real issue lies in understanding how we can integrate it critically into socially useful projects, developing *hybrid intelligence* (Dellermann et al., 2019) oriented towards collectively defined goals. After all, if we demand it as a society, our relationship with GenAI should serve to enrich the cognitive and formative experiences that allow us to grow our individual and collective intelligence.

In this sense, an ethically and pedagogically constructive GenAI cannot be designed to respond assertively, convincingly, pleasantly or seductively to user inputs (or prompts). If it wants to play an emancipatory role, the GenAI must stop presenting itself as if it were a friendly oracle. On the contrary, it must be designed to stimulate reflective thinking, instigating doubt rather than providing apparently infallible and conclusive answers. The close relationship between trust in AI and the erosion of critical judgement, a real transfer of epistemic authority (and therefore of our ability to be intelligent) in advanced automation computing processes, has also been proven by the most recent and diverse research (Gerlich, 2025; Lee et al., 2025; Sturgill, 2025; Tully et al., 2025).

These studies demonstrate how the naive confidence in the potential of AI (effect of the aforementioned *automation bias*), driven in part by the desire to take shortcuts and increase productivity, involves not only students, but also teachers, journalists, creatives and IT programmers. Evidence from this research shows a progressive phenomenon of "intellectual deskilling" and "upskilling inhibition" (a loss of analytical skills and the reduction in opportunities to develop new skills) in frequent users of AI chatbots for learning, asking questions, training and solving problems.

For example, according to the study The Impact of Generative AI on Critical Thinking: Self-Reported Reductions in Cognitive Effort and Confidence

Effects From a Survey of Knowledge Workers (Lee et al., 2025): "Participants reported a tendency to accept AI-generated answers without questioning their validity, illustrating a weakening of individual critical engagement" (p. 7). Consequently, the tendency to relinquish one's cognitive faculties by delegating them to GenAI systems demonstrates excessive confidence in such computational capabilities, risking the production "of a culture of intellectual outsourcing, where students avoid engaging with complexity" (p. 11). However, it is reported that depending on the type of task to be performed, a "cognitive load shift" occurs. In responsible jobs, knowledge workers report that they expend less initial effort (writing, creating, searching for data) but more effort on verification, checking, editing, adaptation ("integration") and management of the generated result. This shift means that less emphasis is placed on creative, analytical and original thinking, which require greater cognitive effort; instead, monitoring and correction phases prevail (p. 18).

The data collected in Gerlich's research on AI Tools in Society: Impacts on Cognitive Offloading and the Future of Critical Thinking (2025) points in the same direction. However, the study adds demographic and educational level variables to explain the tendency to delegate cognitive tasks (memory, decision-making, information retrieval) to AI. As the author states: "Younger participants (17–25) exhibited higher AI tool usage and cognitive offloading, but lower critical thinking scores". In contrast, "older participants (46 and above) showed lower AI tool usage and cognitive offloading, with higher critical thinking scores" (Gerlich, 2025, p. 10).

Further confirmation of the risk to critical thinking in educational and training contexts, specifically in the medical field, can be found in the work of Natali et al. (2025), significantly titled AI-induced Deskilling in Medicine: A Mixed-Method Review and Research Agenda for Healthcare and Beyond. The article points out that the adoption of AI may limit the contexts in which healthcare professionals' experiment, make mistakes, develop independent solutions, and practise "learning by doing". This active learning environment may be eroded if AI intervenes directly in decisions or processes. It refers to the principle that if a skill is not actively used, it can deteriorate ("use it or lose it"). AI that provides "ready-made" solutions may encourage doctors to use their diagnostic skills less, and thus not practise or refine them. In the authors' own words: "In the long run, this inhibition may result in a generation of clinicians who are less prepared to operate without AI assistance, exacerbating concerns about the sustainability of human expertise in medicine" (Natali et al., 2025, p. 2). Finally, the article suggests that the areas that are most difficult to quantify, such as tacit knowledge, clinical judgement and patient communication, are among the most vulnerable to the "inhibition" of new skill acquisition, because AI can replace or discourage the active use of these sophisticated human skills (Natali, 2025, pp. 33–35).

These are just a few more examples of how the skills required to achieve the six learning objectives defined in Bloom's taxonomy can be easily undermined by GenAI applications. More precisely, while students or trainees at the beginning of their careers see the formation of their learning skills profoundly threatened, experienced knowledge workers face the need for a radical shift of those same skills. As remarked in Lee et al. (2025):

> We observed that the use of GenAI tools shifts the knowledge workers' perceived critical thinking effort in three ways. Specifically, for recall and comprehension, the focus shifts from information gathering to information verification. For application, the emphasis shifts from problem-solving to AI response integration. Lastly, for analysis, synthesis, and evaluation, effort shifts from task execution to task stewardship.
>
> (p. 15)

To transform GenAI systems into collaborators, rather than replacements, we must therefore change our pedagogical strategy and work to reorient these systems towards epistemologically emancipatory goals, i.e., goals capable of enriching (augmenting) our cognitive performance.

In light of these changes, training knowledge workers to think critically when working with GenAI should focus on developing skills in information verification, response integration and task stewardship. Training programmes should emphasise the importance of cross-referencing AI outputs, assessing the relevance and applicability of AI-generated content, and continuously refining and guiding AI processes. Additionally, a focus on maintaining foundational skills in information gathering and problem-solving would help workers avoid becoming overreliant on AI (ivi).

In this sense, some alternative AI system projects can be read as critical experiments that seek to reorient technological mediation towards more reflective forms of interaction and knowledge, and thereby contribute to an idea of augmented intelligence, our own. Among the most interesting proposals aimed at countering the prevailing trend by redirecting the use of the same technological tools are applications of "programmed inefficiencies" or what could be defined as an "inhibition protocol" (Fregosi & Cabitza, 2024; Natali et al., 2025).

In line with "undesign" and "machine unlearning" theorists (Pierce, 2014; Widdicks, 2018; Mercuri et al., 2022; Zhang et al., 2023), the aim is to create the technological presuppositions for a reflected choice, opening up a space and time for the deceleration of interaction (a "choice gap" as Tristan Harris would say), and thus immunising against the opposite tendency of the automated acceleration of interactions and the expressive and conceptual homogenisation provided by the patterns of algorithmic repetition (a "mechanised convergence" in the expression of Lee and colleagues).

To this end, then, it becomes useful to circumvent overly smooth human–computer interactions–techniques that conceal the complexity of AI. Introducing elements of uncertainty into the interaction can create "productive friction": by inserting a delay or an additional step, such design choices open up a space for doubt and critical verification. Since it is well known that excessive ease fosters intellectual laziness and dependence, weakening the user's capacity for independent reasoning, friction may serve as a pedagogical counterweight. As Natali et al. (2025) argue, frictional AI resists the smoothness of interaction and instead introduces a productive delay, allowing users to question, verify, and reconsider the system's outputs (Natali et al., 2025, pp. 30–32). For these authors, designing friction is a way to materialise values such as transparency, accountability, and user empowerment within AI-mediated practices (p. 28). This is why, as Fregosi and Cabitza (2024) also remind us, by confronting users with uncertainty and requiring them to engage actively, frictional AI can preserve critical thinking skills (Fregosi & Cabitza, 2024, pp. 2–4), that would otherwise atrophy (Natali et al., 2025, p. 10).

In this sense, instead of responding immediately or (even worse) instead of searching independently by us users what we might be interested in looking for, AI would ask the user for a framework about his request, demanding an analytical proposal before presenting any response. And when answering, instead of defining and narrowing down the scope of the answer, it would ask: *What do you consider to be the most relevant part of this result? Have you checked this information with other sources?* More than just a repository of correct answers, AI should make the user responsible by providing (at least) two alternative and contradictory answers, always accompanied by the corresponding justifications.

The educational function of AI in this context would not be to replace cognitive work, but to provoke it. It would be up to the user, as in a clinical diagnosis or a court judgement, to decide which hypothesis would be the most plausible, appropriate or defensible, integrating this process into their professional, academic or civic practice.

For this to be possible, it is essential to promote a paradigm shift in the way knowledge is created, developed and circulated. This change implies not only the development of more critical interfaces (with *friction* and intellectual *effort* for the user), but also specific educational strategies capable of training users who not only know how to search for information, but above all, who know how to critically interrogate it within a framework of constituted and known references. *Prompt literacy* is not just a technical skill, but an essential epistemological device for reflecting on and questioning the present.

Furthermore, it is essential that technology companies encourage structured review processes for AI-generated content, subject to rigorous human control. This implies that the relevant critical skills are those of the humans called upon to supervise and edit the computational processes of AI services. At the same time, tools should be implemented to highlight the degrees of uncertainty in the answers provided by chatbots, making it clear that these are systems based on calculating probabilities (based on so-called "stochastic parrots", which jeopardise any original result, being impervious to the unknown and unthought). Users must know not only *why* answers are generated one way or another but also be prevented from attributing unwarranted authority to them.

Our human intelligence is enhanced when we critically mediate computational outputs. AI-generated text should be a point of departure for debate, not the endpoint of reasoning. The contemporary challenge is to cultivate pedagogies and work ethics of creative resistance, where error, hesitation, divergence and motivation regain their cognitive value. Only by doing so can we build a cognitive ecosystem where *unconsciousness* or *artificial ignorance* becomes an instrument for improving decisions rather than automating them.

Critical AI literacy is not about *algorithmic aversion*; it is a pedagogy committed to challenging the cultural–economic projects underpinning AI systems, their datasets, infrastructures and algorithmic logics. It's about denaturalising the hypnotic relationship with technological innovation and educating people to question: *who built this system? For what purpose? Whom does it serve or harm? How could there be more transparent AI systems? How could we use technology to challenge intellectual freedom and responsibility?*

Ethical remedies for artificial ignorance: a matter of strategic enveloping

Questioning the "intelligence" of artificial intelligence offers an opportunity to decouple these systems from functions that degrade human cognition and to redefine them around aims that reconnect our lives with society, other species and the environments that sustain us.

The technological conditions already exist for AI to support goals such as reducing energy consumption, but this would require abandoning the extractivist development model sustained by oligarchic agreements, geopolitical competition and the perpetual pursuit of private accumulation. These are crucial challenges which, however, in a fragmented public sphere and a dissociated public opinion, become diluted and obscured by the endless entertainment on digital platforms that claim to make users empowered protagonists. Captured by consumerist imperatives, AI thus follows a trajectory opposite to the much-celebrated ecological transition, becoming co-responsible for the exponential rise in CO_2 emissions.

Beyond the need for political and pedagogical debate on the civilisational aims we wish to restore, it is equally essential to reclaim a richer concept of intelligence. As already noted, reducing intelligence to an automated process of functional optimisation also reduces human beings to mere instruments.

Information disorder, polarised discourse, social detachment and the fragmentation of attention across notifications constitute a structural challenge for the kind of culture and social anthropology being shaped by "dativorous", attention-capturing companies. It is therefore urgent to clarify what kind of intelligence actually operates in the AI systems we use daily. Such clarification would make it more feasible to identify the socio-technical and computational processes that structure their functionalities and affordances, determining interactions, cognition, predispositions and consequences in public and private life, and to articulate ethical and political concerns as well as alternative responses.

By addressing such issues, it becomes easier to identify the process in which such concerns and ethical challenges come into play. For example, according to a recent review of the literature on this topic (Birhane et al., 2021), out of the 100 most cited articles published in the last 15 years in the proceedings of the two most important annual conferences in the sector (NeurIPS and ICML), only two mentioned and discussed the potential harm of the AI applications presented; the remaining 98 did not mention any, therefore eliminating the possibility of discussing them, despite the fact that a lot of the research dealt with socially controversial application areas, such as surveillance and misinformation.

This omission or indifference to the social and human implications can be explained by "technological fetishism" (Baldi & Costa, 2015), subtly reinforced by cinematic narratives, advertising rhetoric and overly specialised knowledge that makes a transdisciplinary epistemic model impossible. The belief in the cognitive and "intelligent" nature of AI stems from an infantilised psychological bias towards the "magical mysteries" of technology (Eco, 1999; Postman, 2002). In fact, its only extraordinary ability is engineering, which reproduces *actions* designed and shaped to achieve predetermined results.

The real AI we know, despite the sensationalist publicity about its advances, does not operate on the basis of a generative, productive intelligence. The philosopher Luciano Floridi insisted on this point in an original way (Floridi, 2023a). For Floridi, AI does not imply any machine intelligence, only computational action ("*agere*"). So, the question that emerges once again is: if machines act by performing tasks and solving problems, independently and without thinking ("*agere sine intelligere*"), if they are not productive and intentional, if they do what they do without any justifiable motivations, how can they be moral? (Floridi, 2023a, p. 48).

Can the non-intelligent machines that dominate the AI scenario be designed to reduce the anthropological costs of automated innovation and produce environmental benefits for their users? Machines are efficient, though not very flexible, they anticipate needs and solve problems even before they arise; however, they force their users to obey them so that they can perform their mechanical work. The most advanced developments in AI, based on the Large Language Model, are still a *syntactic* rather than a *semantic* engine. In this sense, in its unintentional operation, artificial intelligence reveals itself to be an artificial unconsciousness (or artificial ignorance, or even, a socially illiterate intelligence) (Larson, 2021).

Our private and public spaces have been reontologised by the infosphere. The objects and services automated by artificial intelligence systems, those we normally use in our homes, workplaces or to manage interconnected devices, are programmed to respond efficiently to the environment within which they are to be inserted, an environment full of data and sensors designed to interact automatically with what they house, or in other words, with what they "envelop" (Floridi, 2023a, pp. 39–42).

According to Floridi, this reontologisation made operational by the infosphere consists of an "enveloping" of the social environment in its various public and private domains. It is we, then, who create specific environments, the enveloping suited to the characteristics of reproductive and engineering-based AI; an enveloping, then, tailored to AI's predetermined capacity for action.

The robots in Amazon's warehouses are not intelligent, but the aisles, heights of counters, square footage and distances between shelves are. The world surrounding robots is designed to ensure the performance for which robots have been designed. The vacuum cleaner or automated lawn mower need to find prepared floors and gardens for their work to make sense. Car lanes for driverless cars have to be very different from real roads, otherwise the vehicles lose their sense of direction and stability (Floridi, 2023a, pp. 25–26).

Who must adapt to whom? This is the question raised by Floridi. As a society we have a subservient relationship with technological novelties, a provincial attitude that leaves us passive in the face of what the technological market is establishing as the new standard and the new yardstick for our sense of conformity to the world. What the big companies determine as innovation ends up being adopted and integrated into our work and private routines, requiring us to constantly adapt to what these tech companies present under the labels of "optimisation" or "revolutionary". In this sense, our attitude is that of someone waiting to know when and how to comply with a new wave of technological devices and computer architectures. It is our communication that becomes artificial, since we adapt our communicational pragmatics (being plastic and therefore intelligent) to the rigid characteristics of the technologies we encounter (Esposito, 2022).

In a scenario redesigned by the new AI, who should adapt to whom? Do we surrender to technological unconsciousness, or do we strategically redesign our environments so that technology serves us, i.e. adapts to the human way of life we favour? Such processes involve not only the governance of the many social implications of AI (work, privacy, education, environment, power relations), but also the ethics of its use and subsequent planning – both in the design of its functionalities and the infrastructure that supports them.

Projects such as those developed by the company Anthropic, designed to ensure AI Large Language Models grounded in civic responsibility and scientifically verified information, are notable not only for the originality of their methods for reviewing model behaviour and outputs, but also for their effort to define ethical rules and principles (a "constitution") derived from sources such as the Universal Declaration of Human Rights and other AI safety guidelines, which specify how the model should behave. In this sense, the drafting of guidelines conceived and shared across multiple professional profiles ("Constitutional AI") is used to train LLMs like Claude, ensuring that they operate within predefined ethical, legal and safety boundaries, thereby reducing the risk of generating harmful, biased or toxic content (Bai et al., 2022). What remains critical, however, is the fact that these (undoubtedly estimable) projects are the result of private enterprise. Considering the significant public and international impact of these AI models, these "constitutions" should be drafted, guided, applied and federated by public institutions and authorities.

In this sense, some examples of digital infrastructure design in the public interest, and alternatives to algocratic tendencies, are reflected in the policies of transparency, co-design, and accountability that guide the management of AI services in some cities. The *Cities Coalition for Digital Rights* is an example of cities federated together through the sharing of public administration projects and the democratisation of digital services.[2]

Projects of this kind not only make AI records constantly available for public consultation (thus promoting civic trust through transparency) but also create space for suggestions, request, and criticisms from citizens aimed at more inclusive digital services. Yet, in many cases, this socially valuable function of AI is not recognised by institutions, leaving it to organised citizens to assert its strategic importance for the common good. In what follows, we examine several examples of "algo-activism" that attempt from the bottom up to challenge the inertia characterising contemporary digital governance.

Politicising AI: between governance and battles of algorithmic resistance

Working socially and politically to reassert control over digital infrastructures is one of the key aspects of governance that would allow the hierarchies and power relations between political, economic and technological actors to be rebalanced. Such an investment in infrastructural sovereignty would imply revalorising the economic and political autonomy of countries whose infrastructures are currently exploited by the large "dativorous" and parasitic platforms. Politically strengthening the role of public policy in the governance of digital and technological capital would benefit both markets and democracy. In a historical moment marked by a new geopolitical conflict for commercial and military hegemony, information warfare and technological innovation have become the central weapons shaping shifting power relations between opposing blocs (Colon, 2023). In this sense, *another world is possible* insofar as *another Internet* is also possible.

As mentioned in the previous chapter, the concepts of "dismantling" and "infraethics" offer theoretical and practical tools for creating the conditions of possibility necessary to reclaim the common good and moral life. Alternative socio-technical infrastructures and different routines of digital life could indeed support a social reconfiguration of ethics and morality.

The techno-political challenge is therefore to redesign digital services so that they respect and guarantee fundamental democratic and ecological requirements; to put an end to the profiling of user experiences according to the whims and greed of algorithmic power; and to recreate environments that open pathways to renewed relational, epistemic and ethical capacities. Human relationships (with their affective, symbolic and solidaristic dimensions, irreducible and incomputable) can be placed once again at the centre of social life through struggles that politicise the cultural choices shaped by the dismantling and *re*-envelopment of the already mentioned "negative commons".

Based on the analysis of a new microphysics of algorithmic power, and on the results of several studies in the field of artificial intelligence (its instruments and the environments in which it structures experience) scepticism is justified regarding the tendency to conceive our relationship with AI through a typically Hegelian "master–slave" dialectic. In this vision, the *slave* becomes the human subject, compelled to fulfil the obligations dictated by the functionalities of the technology designed by the *Master*, or by the grey eminences of the new mathematical power.

The proposal is to rethink how ethical priorities are framed in the design and implementation of AI systems, promoting a relationship between AI and human intelligences more attuned to the demands of social beings, their environments, and their "ways of life". Ethics, in its political and civilisational implications, comes into play insofar as these concerns are integrated into the design of AI infrastructures and into the reconstruction of the environments that host them, so that computational systems act in ways truly favourable to us.

Achieving such a balance requires, first of all, reflecting on what we genuinely consider a priority for our quality of life; only then can the types of governance, interdisciplinarity and collaboration among researchers with different skills, sensitivities and cultural backgrounds be defined. Equally crucial is the sharing of a common moral vocabulary, words detached from the isolation and fragmentation typical of digital consumption, and decolonised from the competition of all against all, from the gamification of reality, and from assessment systems that are at once persecutory, socially levelling, and psychologically infantilising. Words that must be repoliticised through genuinely aggregating civilising projects (Morozov, 2025).

Some of these counter-trends are emerging, on the one hand, within political activism, whose antagonistic algorithmic perspectives mobilise, albeit in a disaggregated and circumstantial way, new struggles for social justice *in* and *through* the digital space (Söderberg & Maxigas, 2022); on the other hand, in more institutional spheres, new normative designs have been conceived with the intention of rebalancing the power relations between the economic and political actors that make up the constellation of interests affecting the infosphere, i.e.: owners of digital platforms and services, content creators and distributors, public institutions and end users (this is what the European Union's "AI Act" would aim to achieve).

Artificial Intelligence and digital platforms can be oriented towards a logic of social utility. They can be evaluated politically on the basis of metrics other than financial ones. Once we have defined the social, environmental, economic and cultural goals we want to pursue and cultivate (the UN's sustainable development goals could guide the algorithmic design of AI-based projects), it will be decisive to politically redesign (and envelop) the socio-technical space to tell machines how to act in order to achieve our goals, allowing us to better express our qualities, attitudes and needs.

To reach this new horizon of governance and accountability for advanced computer systems, there must also be, as previously discussed, social pressure capable of making these transformations possible. These will be politically, legally and economically incisive if, in parallel, they are instigated by organised sociocultural movements. To politicise the governance of AI, it is therefore pertinent to also reflect on those movements, generally defined as grassroots, which are often decisive in helping to create a discursive agenda and a civic framework on the social issues raised in a sharp manner.

Indeed, there are civic responses to the technologisation of private and public existence, particularly to its "datacratic", technocratic and algocratic drifts. Through more or less formal citizens' movements or specific civic actions, initiatives of "algorithmic resistance" have emerged, often described as "data activism", "info-activism" or "algo-activism". Their targets are the digital instruments that sustain and reproduce specific microphysics of power. By sabotaging, manipulating or re-adapting parts of the functionalities of computational systems engineered by commercial platforms or, in some cases, by public entities, these initiatives aim to interfere in the socio-technical processes of categorisation and differentiation that structure the distribution of opportunities, visibilities and social recognitions. Ultimately, even the very modalities through which citizenship is exercised are increasingly shaped by such algorithmic processes.

The info-communication competencies of digital activists allow them to use the algorithms that drive mainstream platforms for specific objectives, demonstrating their ability to repurpose the "data-greedy" and commercial logics of these systems for alternative ends. Just as the power of data depends on how they are aggregated and interpreted, the power of algorithms originates from the choices made by those who design and apply them. Both data and algorithms respond to certain needs and desires, but under particular circumstances, they can be reappropriated by competent and organised users to achieve objectives different from those previously attributed to them.

Such experiences immunise against a univocal view regarding the infrastructural power of platforms. Shoshana Zuboff (2019), for instance, asserts that data collection and the use of predictive algorithms by corporations in the tech industry represent a means of modifying human behaviour, capable of not only rendering it entirely predictable and controllable but also automated through a "digital order that thrives within things and bodies", transforming individual will into a mechanism of "stimulus-response-reinforcement" and action into conditioned response (Zuboff, 2019, p. 378).

However, an excessive focus on the growing power of platforms risks underestimating or ignoring wiser and more critical digital practices, as well as studies focused on algorithmic resistance movements. Algorithmic activism seeks to translate such practices into political struggle, turning algorithms into a new battleground for social movements (Maly, 2018, 2019).

In this sense, there are tactics of resistance against the major digital platforms that have become the infrastructures of our daily lives. These tactics often take on the characteristics of digital "guerrilla warfare", i.e. techniques of interposition and sabotage within the functioning of such platforms, as well as digitally organised activities to denounce the opaque computer systems that condition the reorganisation of the social (taking up Bruno Latour's definition of *reassembling the social*).

Some types of algorithmic resistance can be easy to carry out. For example, when logging into www.facebook.com/?sk=h_chr, users can force the platform's timeline to display posts chronologically using the "h_chr" command, thus preventing Meta from using its own attention-maximising algorithm by prioritising emotionally divisive content.

Another popular example of combating the structural power of platforms, that doesn't require computer skills, is zoomescaper.com, a website that, in order to criticise the remote working model and the Zoom platform's monopoly on supporting this type of work organisation (Work From Home), offers noise disturbance tools. Users who visit zoomescaper.com can deploy noisy audio applications that they insert into Zoom meetings. In simple terms, the site provides a set of options that users can modify so that they can insert the sounds of *construction work, crying children, barking dogs, ambulances with sirens on*, etc. into the middle of conversations. The service is presented by its creators as a technique to sabotage the audio stream, making their presence unbearable for others (Lavigne, 2021; Mueller, 2021).

Other scholars working at the intersection of social movements and media studies have addressed the ways in which activists and algorithms become mutually entangled in protest contexts. Galis and Neumayer (2016), in their study of digital protests in Greece and Sweden, introduced the concept of "cyber-material detournement", an *amphibious* notion to highlight the need to act simultaneously between alien habitats (both physical and conceptual) and to combine alliances between activists and non-human actors (such as algorithmic agents).

Kant (2020), for example, describes users who are critically involved in "manoeuvring within, against and through algorithmic anticipation" (2020, p. 215) as "algorithmic tacticians". In other cases, the "tactical algorithms" used in social media leverage the characteristics of computational automation for more disruptive political ends, attempting to turn an antagonistic democratic struggle into "code" (Crawford, 2016). As such, algorithmic antagonism implies resistance not only through the algorithm itself, but as a "composite of human-algorithm relations" (Amoore, 2020) to be contextualised within specific social, economic and political conditions of creation and use.

From this perspective, we are approaching a more comprehensive political theory, which no longer sees the digital as a lever and instrument for waging social-political struggles, but as an expressive and operational terrain of new powers. Algorithmic antagonism must recognise the many microphysics of computational power present in the digital space, questioning, for example, the socio-mathematical genesis of algorithms, the process of constituting data, the problems they solve, but also verifying the damage they can cause as automated practices of providing knowledge and decisions are institutionalised. As such, the algorithmic struggle results not only in a concern for the injustice embedded in the code, but also for the way algorithms emerge and operate in society in a broader and more structural way.

These are, therefore, experiences of tension between socio-technical regimes and digital activists, struggles aimed at exercising a democratic "agonism", capable of exposing the constantly shifting devices of contestation.

The tactical nature of algorithmic struggle, as outlined, can indeed support the political theory conceptualised by Chantal Mouffe (2005), that is, a democratic "agonism" that doesn't seek to achieve stable control over social conflicts but offers an acceptance of the contestability of one's own political position. An openness to constant dialectic, then, which creates "adversaries", not "enemies", in favour of a continuous struggle for a different idea of social justice. From this perspective, the democratic ethos of algorithmic activism would be based on a political dispute that aims to make visible those technological structures that are part of agonism, but which can go unnoticed because they are an active part of the "mediamorphosis" that involves relations between humans and platformised culture.

However, we may ask ourselves: can such digital tactics provide an alternative course for the creation of new platforms and infrastructures, designing effective algorithms to act transparently and democratically in everyday, social and political life? Can individual and collective actions based primarily on tactics play an important role in socio-political and economic issues related to the dispute over sovereignty over technological resources?

In search of a political theory that goes beyond mere tactics

Experiences of algorithmic resistance find one of their inspiring theoretical foundations in the notion of "tactics". In this sense, it is useful to end by reflecting on the heuristics of such a resource, both conceptual and practical. To this purpose, it is significant to consider it through its dialectical relationship with the other conceptual and operational pole that determines its framework: that of "strategy". It is with Michel de Certeau, in his *L'invention du quotidien* (1990), that we have an in-depth reflection on these two dimensions of cultural and political experience. He distinguished political actions and cultural practices according to the distribution of power resources (something very similar to Bourdieusian "capitals") among other actors and social groups. These actions and practices, according to the author, are usually conceived and operationalised on the basis of the positions they occupy in the social space and the political and cultural interests they pursue and are thus divided into "strategies" and "tactics".

The first (strategies) would be those implemented by government institutions, political authorities and companies that pursue objectives consistent with reinforcing and reproducing a certain distribution of privileges and social opportunities. The latter (tactics) would be conducted by a heterogeneous class of individuals who, although moving within spaces and coordinates already predetermined by the strategies, would follow alternative needs and propensities that are irreducible to the guidelines established by the former.

Strategies organise and set the rules of the game and can base their objectives and actions on medium and long-term programmes. Tactics, however, react to these rules of the game by trying to adapt them to their own needs. To achieve these results, tactics that oppose strategies must disguise their actions within the social expectations guided by strategies, circumvent dominant interests and evade more favourable conditions in rapid times and interstitial place – contexts of local and contingent readjustment of everyday life.

By comparing the matrices and grammars of these behaviours, de Certeau wanted to emphasise the creativity of many everyday *arts de faire*, individual and collective practices of resistance against the dominant guidelines dictated by hegemonic interests, within a horizon of meaning that is nevertheless colonised by the relations of forces and the rhetoric expressed by those who manage the devices of social valorisation (in the economic, technological, educational, media, political fields, etc.). Tactics and stratagems that don't go as far as inverting power relations or even designing structural alternatives, but only create temporarily autonomous islands of counterculture.

Forty years after the publication of *L'invention du quotidien*, we can consider the distinction between strategies and tactics to be increasingly blurred. Not in terms of the distribution and hierarchisation of power, but in terms of the phenomenology of its exercise. In fact, we are witnessing a similarity between the exercise of the two practices, since the contrastive modalities of tactics, with their instantaneity and adaptability, increasingly resemble the actions of hegemonic strategies. As already mentioned in relation to the *pre*-mediation context, we are increasingly faced with government policies and media communications based on the constant appeal to the "state of crisis" and the "emergency"; in this way, the power dynamics that guide strategies have acquired the rhizomatic characteristics of tactics, at least this is the impression we get from trying to glimpse the rationality of contemporary governmentalities. As described above, the new grey eminences also base their strategies on generating a multiplicity of concerns and uncertainties that undermine the "ontological security" of life in society.

If, on the one hand, we are witnessing political communication focused on the persistent transmission of anxieties about the most diverse social adversities, represented as incumbent threats, on the other hand, we are faced with an administration of political and economic power cornered by interests perceived as transcendent and unintelligible in the face of practical common sense. There is permanent socio-political uncertainty, where the techniques for exercising hegemony become less predictable, oscillating between urgencies and attempts to respond to them in a logic of just-in-time pretexts.

The parameters that define the perimeters of intervention, both on the side of those who have the prerogative of more profitable symbolic and material capital, and those who intend to resist them and sway the imbalances of power, are therefore shifting and unstable, making it difficult to develop coordinated and lasting attitudes. Also within the governance of digital platforms, which guide the criteria and styles of our sociability and creativity, we are faced with a constant change in the rules of the terms of use, as well as the codes that enhance their functionalities (Poell et al., 2021).

In this sense, "infoactivism" is in a double condition of *minority* to the administrators and creators of the algorithmic powers of the platforms in common use. Tactics are not only trapped in a dynamic of reaction to the persistence of power structures that are difficult to question, but they also lose the possibility of cultivating and articulating technological competences of resistance to dynamise actions in the medium and long term.

This discrepancy brings us back to a general problem of political theory. Counter-hegemonic struggles should consist of an organised political design that aims for structural changes or the creation of alternative structures (economic, technological, institutional, environmental, educational, political, etc.), broadening the range of fundamental instruments and resources to increase social consensus on the needs and desires to carry out such transformations. However, in the economy of contemporary counter-hegemonic struggles, there prevails an almost resigned attitude to defending micro-instances, specific dimensions of everyday life and identity issues that are not integrated into a horizon of politically broader practices and ideologies. The ambition of a socio-political rescue also involves the revindication and construction of alternative communicative infrastructures, with different programming rules and a diverse political economy of reference to sustain them. Transforming tactics into strategies requires a new material and cultural context for communication and info-diversity.

The daily *arts de faire*, also in a platformised context, undoubtedly play a role in survival and democratic vitality, but they are not politically relevant if they remain in a fragmented and punctual operational dimension. Fortunately, within the dominant digital platforms we do come across digital "detox" movements, algorithmic decolonisation, activism promoted by minorities, environmentalist struggles, sharing experiences and information that are important for personal and collective enrichment. Although most of the information traffic is channelled more towards polarised attitudes and is captured in iterative engagement practices, we can't neglect those interactive dimensions that are less diffuse, but no less cognitively, ethically, and affectively relevant.

However, while laudable and necessary, movements that try to bridge and overcome invisibilities and political inequalities through punctual and dispersed tactics fail to trigger collective processes capable of challenging the transformation or renegotiating the balance of the hegemonic axes of the political order, or even the policies of the dominant platforms. The risk is, once again, that they will only remain in the cultural terrain ploughed by the neoliberal logics of group narcissism and identity gratification. It is when these movements (heterogeneous in their identities, structures and statutes) organise themselves and recognise common causes that they will then be able to leverage convergent social practices capable of building ethical consensus on the need to create new shared mediation structures and thus provide a scenario, an *instituting power*, for establishing new rules and criteria of representativeness (opposed to those that reflect financial logics) for the controversies of democratic life (Esposito, 2021).

Notes

1 *IE University research reveals 1 in 2 Europeans want to replace national MPs with robots*. In https://www.ie.edu/university/news-events/news/ie-university-research-reveals-1–2-europeans-want-replace-national-mps-robots/.
2 https://citiesfordigitalrights.org/.

References

Amoore, L. (2020). *Cloud ethics*. Duke University Press.
Aneesh, A. (2009). Global labor: Algocratic modes of organization. *Sociological Theory 27*(4). https://doi.org/10.1111/j.1467-9558.2009.01352.x
Araujo, T., Helberger, N., Kruikemeier, S., & Vreese, C. H. (2020). In AI we trust? Perceptions about automated decision-making by artificial intelligence. *AI & Society, 35*(3), 611–623. https://doi.org/10.1007/s00146-019-00931-w
Bai, Y., Kadavath, S., Kundu, S., Askell, A., Kernion, J., Jones, A.,…, & Kaplan, J. (2022). Constitutional ai: Harmlessness from ai feedback. https://arxiv.org/abs/2212.08073, 2212
Baldi, V., & Costa, M. F. (2015). IPhone: pedaço de carne suculento. *Observatorio (OBS*), 9*(4), 159–171. https://doi.org/10.15847/obsOBS942015883
Barthes, R. (1957). *Mythologies*. Seuil.

Bauman, Z. (2006). *Liquid times: Living in an age of uncertainty*. Polity.

Birhane, A., Kalluri, P., Card, D., Agnew, W., Dotan, R., & Bao, M. (2021). The values encoded in machine learning research. arXiv – arXiv2106.15590v1. https://doi.org/10.48550/arXiv.2106.15590

Bloom, B. S., Engelhart, M. D., Furst, E. J., Hill, W. H., & Krathwohl, D. R. (1956). *Taxonomy of educational objectives: The classification of educational goals. Handbook 1: Cognitive domain*. Longman.

Brown, W. (2015). *Undoing the demos: Neoliberalism's stealth revolution*. Zone Book.

Cabitza, F., Campagner, A., & Simone, C. (2021). The need to move away from agential-AI: Empirical investigations, useful concepts and open issues. *International Journal of Human-Computer Studies*, *155*, 102696.

Colon, D. (2023). *La guerre de l'information: Les États à la conquête de nos esprits*. Éditions Tallandier.

Connock, A., & Stephen, A. (2021). We invited an AI to debate its own ethics in the Oxford Union – What it said was startling. *The Conversation – Oxford University*, 2021. https://theconversation.com/we-invited-an-ai-to-debate-its-own-ethics-in-the-oxford-union-what-it-said-was-startling-173607

Crary, J. (2022). *Scorched earth: Beyond the digital age to a post-capitalist world*. Verso.

Crawford, K. (2016). Can an algorithm be agonistic? Ten scenes from life in calculated publics. *Science, Technology, & Human Values*, *41*(1), 77–92. https://doi.org/10.1177/0162243915589635

Crawford, K. (2021). *Atlas of AI: Power, politics, and the planetary costs of artificial intelligence*. Yale University Press.

Danaher, J. (2016). The threat of algocracy: Reality, resistance and accommodation. *Philosophy and Technology*, *29*(3), 245–268. https://doi.org/10.1007/s13347-015-0211-1

de Certeau, M. (1990). *L'invention du quotidien*. Gallimard.

Debord, G. (1990). *Comments on the society of the spectacle*. Verso.

Dellermann, D., Ebel, P., Söllner, M., & Leimeister, J. M. (2019). Hybrid intelligence. *Business & Information Systems Engineering (BISE)*, *61*(5), 637–643.

Eagleman, D. (2020). *Livewired: The inside story of the ever-changing brain*. Penguin Random House.

Eco, E. (1999). *Kant e o Ornitorrinco*. Difel.

Esposito, R. (2021). *Istituzione*. Il Mulino.

Esposito, E. (2022). *Artificial communication. How algorithms produce social intelligence*. MIT Press.

Floridi, L. (2023a). *The ethics of artificial intelligence. Principles, challenges, opportunities*. Oxford University Press.

Floridi, L. (2023b). *The green and the blue: Naive ideas to improve politics in the digital age*. Wiley-Blackwell.

Foucault, M. (2004). *Naissance du Biopolitique*. Seul.

Fregosi, C., & Cabitza, F. (2024). A frictional design approach: Towards judicial AI and its possible applications. *Workshops at the Third International Conference on Hybrid Human-Artificial Intelligence (HHAI)*. June, 10–14. Malmö, Sweden.

Galis, V., & Neumayer, C. (2016). Laying claim to social media by activists: A cyber-material détournement. *Social Media+ Society, 2*(3). https://doi.org/10.1177/2056305116664360

Gerlich, M. (2025). AI tools in society: Impacts on cognitive offloading and the future of critical thinking. *Societies, 15*(1), 6. https://doi.org/10.3390/soc15010006

Habermas, J. (1992). *Between facts and norms. Contributions to a discourse theory of law and democracy*. MIT Press.

Harari, Y. N. (2018). *21 Lessons for the 21st century*. Spiegel & Grau, Jonathan Cape.

Heemsbergen, L., Treré, E., & Pereira, G. (2022). Introduction to algorithmic antagonisms: Resistance, reconfiguration, and renaissance for computational life. *Media International Australia, 183*(1), 3–15. https://doi.org/10.1177/1329878X221086042

Heidegger, M. (1968). *What is called thinking?* Harper & Row.

Kahneman, D., Rosenfield, A. M., Gandhi, L., & Blaser, T. (2016). NOISE: How to overcome the high, hidden cost of inconsistent decision making. *Harvard Business Review, 94*(10), 38–46.

Kant, T. (2020). *Making it personal: Algorithmic personalization, identity, and everyday life*. Oxford University Press.

Larson, E. (2021). *The myth of artificial intelligence. Why computers can't think the way we do*. Harward University Press.

Lavigne, S. (2021). *Zoom escaper*. https://zoomescaper.com

Lee, Hao-Ping (Hank) et al. (2025). The impact of generative AI on critical thinking: Self-reported reductions in cognitive effort and confidence effects from a survey of knowledge workers. *Proceedings of the 2025 CHI Conference on Human Factors in Computing Systems*, 1–22.

Magalhães, J. C., & Couldry, N. (2021). Giving by taking away: Big Tech, data colonialism and the reconfiguration of social good. *International Journal of Communication, 15*(2021), 343–362.

Maly, I. (2018). Algorithmic populism and algorithmic activism. *Diggit Magazine*. https://www.diggitmagazine.com/articles/algorithmic-populism-activism

Maly, I. (2019). New right metapolitics and the algorithmic activism of Schild & Vrienden. *Social Media+ Society, 5*(2). https://doi.org/10.1177/2056305119856700

Mercuri, S., Khraishi, R., Okhrati, R., Batra, D., Hamill, C., Ghasempour, T., & Nowlan, A. (2022). *An introduction to machine unlearning*. arXiv. https://arxiv.org/abs/2209.00939

Morozov, E. (2025). *AI future*. Boston Review.

Mouffe, C. (2005). *On the political*. Routledge.

Mueller, G. (2021). *Breaking things at work: The luddites are right about why you hate your job*. Verso.

Natali, C., Marconi, L., & Dias Duran, L. D. (2025). AI-induced deskilling in medicine: A mixed-method review and research agenda for healthcare and beyond. *Artificial Intelligence Review, 58*, 356. https://doi.org/10.1007/s10462-025-11352-1

Pierce, J. (2014). Undesigning interaction. *Interactions*, 21(4). https://doi.org/10.1145/2626373

Poell, T., Brooke, D. B., & Duffy, E. (2021). *Platforms and cultural production*. Polity.

Postman, N. (2002). *O fim da educação. Redefinindo o valor da educação*. Relógio D'Água.

Ranganathan, A., & Ye, X. M. (2026, February 9). AI doesn't reduce work—It intensifies it. *Harvard Business Review*. https://hbr.org/2026/02/ai-doesnt-reduce-work-it-intensifies-it

Scholz, R. W. (1983). *Decision making under uncertainty: Cognitive decision research, social interaction, development and epistemology*. Elsevier.

Sen, P., & Ganguly, D. (2020). Towards socially responsible AI: Cognitive bias-aware multi-objective learning. *Proceedings of the AAAI Conference on Artificial Intelligence, 34*(03), 2685–2692. https://doi.org/10.1609/aaai.v34i03.5654

Shin, D. (2020). How do users interact with algorithm recommender systems? The interaction of users, algorithms, and performance. *Computer Human Behavior, 109*, 106344. https://doi.org/10.1016/j.chb.2020.106344

Shin, D. (2021a). The effects of explainability and causability on perception, trust, and acceptance: Implications for explainable AI. *International Journal of Human-Computer Studies, 146*, 102551. https://doi.org/10.1016/j.ijhcs.2020.102551

Shin, D. (2021b). Embodying algorithms, enactive artificial intelligence and the extended cognition: You can see as much as you know about algorithm. *Journal of Information Science,* 0165551520985495. https://doi.org/10.1177/0165551520985495

Sloterdijk, P. (2018). *What happened in the 20th century?* Polity Press.

Söderberg, J., & Maxigas (2022). *Resistance to the current: The dialectics of hacking*. MIT Press.

Sturgill, A. (2025). Unlocking the link between generative AI confidence and critical thinking skills. *Center for Engaged Learning* (*blog*). March, 2025. https://www.centerforengagedlearning.org/unlocking-the-link-between-generative-ai-confidence-and-critical-thinking-skills/

Supiot, A. (2015). *La Gouvernance par les Nombres*. Fayard.

Tironi, M., Chilet, M., Marín, C. U., & Hermansen, P. (Eds.). (2023). *Design for more-than-human futures: Towards post-anthropocentric worlding*. Taylor & Francis.

Tully, S. M., Longoni, C., & Appel, G. (2025). Lower artificial intelligence literacy predicts greater AI receptivity. *Journal of Marketing, 0*(0). https://doi.org/10.1177/00222429251314491

van Dijck, J., Poell, T., & de Waal, M. (2018). *The platform society*. Oxford University Press.

Vicente, P. N. (2023). *Os Algoritmos e Nós*. Fundação Francisco Manuel dos Santos.

Vygotskij, L. S. (1978). *Mind in society: The development of higher psychological processes*. Harvard University Press.

Westberg, M., Zelvelder, A. E., & Najjar, A. (2019). A historical perspective on cognitive science and its influence on XAI research. In Calvaresi, D. et al. (Eds.), *International workshop on explainable, transparent autonomous agents and multi-agent systems*, 205–219. Springer.

Widdicks, K. V., Ringenson, T., Pargman, D., Kuppusamy, V., & Lago, P. (2018). *Undesigning the Internet: An exploratory study of reducing everyday Internet connectivity*. In "ICT4S2018. 5th International Conference on Information and Communication Technology for Sustainability", pp. 384–397.

Zhang, H., Nakamura, T., Isohara, T., & Sakurai, K. (2023). A review on machine unlearning. *SN Computer Science, 4*(4), 337.

Zuboff, S. (2019). *The age of surveillance capitalism: The fight for a human future at the new frontier of power*. Profile Books.

3 Beyond Atomising Pedagogies and the Machinery of Human Capital

Introduction

The previous chapters have repeatedly emphasised the interdependence between media environments, technological infrastructures, multimedia languages, digital interfaces, interaction design, cognitive and perceptual habits, forms of sociality, modes of political aggregation and the transmission and circulation of knowledge. Furthermore, as highlighted throughout the book, these dimensions of social experience are embedded in economic, political and cultural interests and values that orient their development. A crucial aspect concerns the pedagogical and epistemological policies that reflect a specific vision of what is considered important to know and to value: an ideologically supported vision of how to classify and hierarchise the social world and of what should be invested in to extract benefits within it.

For this reason, this chapter aims to outline an analysis of these intersections, starting from the symbolic infrastructure represented by knowledge and the pedagogical dimension (which constantly overlaps with the material dimension of technologies and their uses).

Studies on the educational challenges for the 21st century usually converge, in the scientific literature guiding and supporting institutional reforms in the field of education, on the use of a language and taxonomy that promote the transmission of logical and operational skills, the development of computer and technology skills for solving problems, the definition of aims and suitable methodologies to achieve them, and an assessment system based on the numerical ranking of the different performances.

Training programmes and their pedagogies of reference conceive learning contexts as fields where to forge agonistic spirits and encourage competition with the aim of building effective CVs for a future career in close dependence with market demands. The ethics underlying this approach are honestly presented (i.e. firmly presented) as those that can offer promising paths towards excellence and meritocracy. If it is useful for the market, then knowledge has a value and, in this sense, all students are workers *in pectore*.

DOI: 10.4324/9781003765431-4

An emblematic example of governments' diversion of the education system is the normative framework of the European programme Erasmus+, which fosters research and intervention activities in the area of training programmes. In fact, in its latest version (for 2013–2020), all programmes linked to formal and informal education were standardised under the same label, summarised by the keyword "employability". Paradoxically, whoever wished to research the ideological distortion of the concept of education as an end in itself had to apply for funding from the same Erasmus+ programme.[1] This framework, in turn, mirrors an economics-based idolatry that unintentionally came through in the European Commission document signed by Jacques Delors in 1995, *Livre blanc sur l'éducation et la formation. Enseigner et Aprendre. Vers la Société Cognitive*. In this document, the notion of *human capital* marked the idea of education proposed to be successful in life and be able to compete with the other continents.

Therefore, we can ask ourselves: can there be a contemporary pedagogy that is not based on a teaching and assessment system shaped by the utilitarian logic of the market? Can pedagogy be socially significant by fostering an individualistic culture of performance and measurement as criteria for evaluating training processes? Can pedagogy be emancipatory if it promotes a measuring logic as a criterion to assess training and knowledge processes? Are there learning experiences not rooted in disciplinary and monocultural education models? Before continuing to analyse the implications of this educational landscape, it is important to explore some of its historical and cultural roots and to check whether this educational context radicalises a previously outlined epistemological path that has always operated within Western societies.

The Genealogy and Institutionalisation of *Homo Educandus*

If we take a close look at the logic through which the education system is conceived as a battery of codified instruments to equip students with the necessary skills for adult and working life, we see at its core an institutional device that has existed in Western culture for a long time. It was the scholar Ivan Illich, a precursor to research on the vernacular epistemologies implicit in the everyday practices of marginal cultures (inside and outside the West), who recovered the institutionalisation of those education practices through the figure of the *Homo educandus*, a psychological, historical and cultural entity made up in 16th-century Europe, according to which all individuals would need to be educated by pedagogical protocols that institutions had previously agreed on. According to this Christian-derived conception, all human beings always have been and always will be *Homo educandus*, with needs and wants that only education professionals know and can meet and correct.

For Illich, these needs were initially created by ecclesiastical institutions, so that they could consolidate and legitimate their own status as soul administrators and regulators of assistance services, determining the needs and lacks of *Homo educandus* as if these were "anthropological universals", i.e. men were naturally unable to autonomously understand and learn about the things they needed and how to address them.[2]

Pedagogy based on individual defectiveness, on the scarcity of cognitive and social resources, is, according to Illich, an ideological construction whose historicity was never researched. This reinforces its indisputability, as if it had never started in a specific context but were instead a precondition, an *a priori* of all human practices and experiences. Do children actually need education systems to learn how to walk, talk, socialise? Did young people learn at school how to be nomads, how to farm the land, raise cattle, make and handle tools, build and inhabit places or manage resources to deal with the everyday dimension of their context of reference? In the different texts gathered in *La perte des sens* (2004), Illich explains how pedagogical concepts cannot be applied when learning how to use vernacular skills. For him, to think that man is *educandus* by nature, that his well-being – in fact, his entire existence – depends on education systems, is a huge misconception. Therefore, for Illich, the sphere of education is an ideological artifice that fuelled the belief that human beings were invariably subjected to formal learning practices, socially conceived within a set of peculiar institutions whose prototype would be the *Alma Mater Ecclesia*. Hence, the education system inherits and emulates catechism, with its disciplinary practices based on truths contained in the – religious or school – book, which allowed (the Christian or *educandus*) to attain salvation.

The verb *to educate*, whose Latin etymology refers to the mother's role of feeding and breastfeeding the *in-fant*, i.e. the one who does not know how to speak (*educat nutrix*, the feeder educates), dates back to the Judeo-Christian teleological fable that permeates Western culture, where: everything that represents the past is seen as ignorance, absence, injustice; what represents the present is seen as a remedy that mends through research, progress and revolution; and what represents the future is perceived as that which redeems and saves for good.

This pedagogical and institutional system, besides inducing the depreciation of all vernacular learning processes, is historically based on the passivity and opacity encouraged and exhorted in learning individuals, since their needs are exclusively defined and fulfilled by education professionals. Educational institutions, Illich recalls, would then be responsible not only for defining the weaknesses and shortages of men's educational resources, but also, by turning them into problems, finding solutions to them in curriculum formats.

However, the social history of *Homo educandus* is not the same as the history of education. The first refers directly to the *educational paradigm* that made it possible to justify the social construct of education. The second is based on research into the relationships between the sphere of education and the broader ideology of a given society, together with the historical analysis of those relationships, through which it may be possible to understand a hitherto unknown aspect of the history of *Homo oeconomicus*.

In fact, this profile was also constructed around the ideology of the shortage of material resources. In Illich's view, education as an institution assumes that each human being is born as an isolated individual into a contractual society that should be understood before it can be directly lived and experienced. In another collection of studies dedicated to the historical and cultural roots of the myths of modernity, *In the Mirror of the Past. Lectures and Addresses, 1978–1990*, Illich (1992) calls for pedagogists to conduct comparative studies between the history of education and the history of economics and mentalities, challenging education scholars to explore the pre-existing and contemporary alternatives to the educational paradigm of *Homo educandus*, just as Elie Halévy and Karl Polanyi did in the context of economic history and anthropology.

These studies would allow to re-examine educational aims and methods and would rescue non-formal, participatory teaching-learning practices, situated in context, and focused on valuing prior knowledge and experiences, as well as mentorship in the exploration of new training projects. To follow up on the challenges pointed out by Illich, who anticipated and innovated the way of analysing the various political and epistemological devices making up Western modernity, we should start by questioning the symbolic and performative nature of the institutional discourses that sustain the definitions of what is important to learn and know in a given historical context, recovering their relationships and implications with those other public discourses that feed common sense.

The utilitarian logic of educational standardisation

As mentioned in the beginning of this book, the renewal of contemporary training institutions follows the pace of companies starting up, rather than research into cognitive, affective and socio-environmental processes associated with learning. Furthermore, the socio-historical processes that interest these institutions are not those that are reflected in the psychosocial conditions of the new generations, in the balance of family organisations, in the social ties that make up the intellectual flourishing of students and teachers, or in their horizons of political and moral expectations. The concerns of educational institutions refer to other demands that go beyond the complexity of social life, which also affects those involved in educational processes. On the contrary, the various teaching-learning programmes seem to be increasingly consolidating a logic and *ethos* that frames contemporary education as an "incubator" for flexible minds and hands for (rigidly precarious) jobs tailored to companies and start-ups.

In this sense, the current pedagogical model, with its incessant categorisation systems reflected in the processes of seriation, admission, assessment and evaluation, which at the same time involve students, teachers and educational institutes, reveals itself to be a system that aims to legitimise prescriptive training practices colonised by accounting and administrative logics.

The algorithmic governance of management and administrative processes, the "targeting" and "matching" systems provided by *algocracy*, have gradually been colonising the realm of pedagogy with their categorisation systems (in the ranking, admission, appreciation and evaluation processes) subtly transformed into prescriptive models. This interference in and conditioning of the sphere of education issue from a public discourse determined by a set of rhetorics and beliefs in the progressive value of education, understood as a meritocratic workshop whose pillars of reference would be (as will be seen in what follows) *human capital*, the *teaching of competencies* and the *standardised evaluation of performances*, with employability and/or entrepreneurship as their collectively recognised goal. An emblematic proof of this ideological frame of reference is found in a 1997 OECD report on education, *The Definition and Selection of Key Competencies*, where relational skills (*The ability to relate well to others*) are considered key to economic success:

> This first key competency allows individuals to initiate, maintain and manage personal relationships with, for example, personal acquaintances, colleagues and customers. Relating well is not only a requirement for social cohesion but, increasingly, for economic success.
>
> (p. 12)

Another critical aspect, which increases the weight of economic and functionalist normativity in contemporary education, is the insinuation of the culture of quantification as a new value system within human activities. In the digital, competitive and global age in which we live, numbers tend to be imposed as the measure of all things. We are witnessing a regime of numerical morality, where "everything is quantified, counted, measured, weighed, computed, ordered, categorised, catalogued, in order to make objectives, goals, evaluations, judgements, choices, discriminations, impositions, verdicts" (Santos & Soares, 2022, p. 10).

We are not only surrounded by numbers that aim to guide our practices, but also:

> we start producing reports, statistics, polls, surveys, rankings, ratings, tops, templates, scales, algorithms, graphs, formulas, models, matrices, averages, controls, surveillance [...]. Numbers are a new *doxa*, a new belief, and even a new determinism.
>
> (Santos & Soares, 2022, p. 10)

In this sense, we need to question the omnipresence, omnipotence and omniscience acquired by numbers, question the oracular and normative power we give them, as well as the concealment, disregard and devaluation of everything that is incalculable, starting with the political notions of equality, right or integrity, as well as the psychosocial notions of recognition, gratitude, reward or decorum and honour. The transition from analogue to digital seems to have cancelled out the importance of everything that is not numerable; it has given us a cognitive sensitivity to things that sees them only in terms of their possible numerical order. The perverse transformation of society into an "evaluative society" is a reduction of reality to a ciphered evaluation.

Referring back to Michel Foucault's *Les Mots et les Choses* (translated into English with the title *The Order of Things*), on the epistemological conditions of modern rationality, we could look at the foundations of contemporary episteme and the pillars on which the edifice of our thinking and acting is built as "The Order of Numbers" or "Les Numeraux et le Choses".

If, for example, systems to evaluate learning (in fact, it is the "learning contexts", which make these systems possible, that should be evaluated) were not based on a quantitative assessment, we could start to evaluate qualitative processes such as the capacity for reflection and self-reflection, the thought-through correction of one's own mistakes, the cooperation in solving issues discussed, the research of different strategies to approach problems or the dimension of problematising one's own pedagogical method that guides one's own cognitive and learning experience (Morin, 2003).

However, replacing quantitative assessment leads us back to the competitive mercantile strategy, where efficiency in *problem solving* is awarded to the detriment of training activities focusing on the psychosocial performance of *learning to learn*. While the purpose of reflexive education is to critically understand reality, in order to understand its limits and change it, the approach coupled to the development of skills that are profitable in the market assumes that the existing reality is a fact to which one must adapt (Sandel, 2020).

By praising the values inscribed in the acquisition of specialised and commercially profitable skills, the ideology of merit suggests that only those who accept the world as it is – and therefore have to modify themselves, since changing the context is not an option – are truly worthy of recognition. Whereas social conflict feeds on collective action, meritocracy is sustained by individual initiative. The first pursues common aims that can encompass society as a whole, while the logic of merit conceives social progress as a natural effect of the sum of individual cases of success.

In fact, there is no longer any aspect of human life that is not evaluated in economic terms of human capital, competition, valuation, ROI (*return of investment*), etc.: neoliberalism thus becomes "as an order of normative reason that [...] takes shape as a governing rationality extending a specific formulation of economic values, practices, and metrics to every dimension of human life" (Brown, 2015, p. 30). In this sense, the "human capital's constant and ubiquitous aim, whether studying, interning, working, planning retirement or reinventing itself in a new life, is to entrepreneurialise its endeavour, appreciate its value, and increase its rating or ranking" (ivi, p. 36).

As mentioned, the practice of assessment at (secondary and higher) education institutions is based on systems of verification presented as being effective and objective, since they result in exact numbers that summarise and mirror the merit of students in knowing the correct answers in exams (many of which consist of tests). Knowing the answers, in the utilitarian sense of getting the top grade, is more important than endeavouring to understand, delve deeper, explore different ways of reasoning or raising questions. As the physicist and philosopher Heinz von Foerster mentioned in his *Observing Systems*, published in 1984, students are challenged to be banal and predictable, and are encouraged to reject hermeneutic stimuli, since to be successful, they should match to the prerequisites.

Adapting to this numerical order once again leads to quantitative conformism, in other words, a new social order that is morally justified by classification systems. It's no coincidence that part of contemporary technophilia is justified and materialised through an idea of intelligence based on the speed of responses and the optimisation of functional performance.

It's important to emphasise that tests as final exams are not attacked here, but rather their standardisation as a shortcut to reduce the complexity of any evaluation process, thus avoiding other possible systems. Furthermore, tests are often the best solution to respond to a pedagogical system conceived in favour of competition and where the programmes taught pile up and overlap in short periods of time, boiling down to a list of notions. Finally, the paradox that undermines the assumptions of the pedagogical strategies in question: the same education institutions are externally assessed and one of the performance criteria is the number of students assessed per year (and, whenever possible, their integration in the labour market and their success in working life).

There is a common thread between choices, institutional definitions and social discourses that shape interests and sensitivities. The social and economic values proposed or proscribed by government bodies end up permeating a large part of the discursive *ethos* of contemporary society and vice versa. In fact, the hierarchy of social classifications is a result of the representations and public rhetorics that justify it in a tautological way.

Whoever defines the definitions, that is, whoever manages to frame the representations, acquires (whether legitimate or illegitimate) the social power to mould and dominate the reality of what is being represented. As Pierre Bourdieu explained, the power of authorised language comes through in the implicit collective recognition of this permission to officially – and, therefore, legitimately – speak and represent. For Bourdieu, the "mystery of the ministry" symbolises this magic and performative power of language, when it is institutionally authorised, but socially permitted (Bourdieu, 1997).

The broad consensus on the social role that education should play is based on that set of institutionally legitimated and shared obvious facts that make up common sense. While for Ivan Illich these facts (dating back to the 16th century) revolved around the idea that human beings were necessarily defective (to redeem the original sin), current European training programmes emphasise the challenges of meritocratic excellence, summed up in the competition for employability (to invest in the *right* future, that of the global market).

Reclaiming alternative epistemologies

Scholars such as Ludwig Wittgenstein (1969) and Bruno Latour (1999), at very different moments in time, never ceased to point out that epistemological discussions about classification methods and systems should not overlook the fact that every instrument of knowledge also takes on functions that are not of pure knowledge. The representation of a pure and disinterested epistemology, both in its genealogy and in its practical repercussions, is an illusion. However, there are (ethically oriented) illusions that can also mobilise towards more ambitious and unpredictable epistemic practices, i.e. those that result from recognising the promiscuity with the social world that surrounds them, stimulating antibodies against the prepotency of a "logocentrism" that aims to separate the formation of knowledge itself from the context and practical experience of its exercise.

Conventional ways of presenting and producing knowledge, the ways of expressing its aims and methodologies, are always anchored in the social conditions of its production and reproduction; in this sense, as Bourdieu analysed, taxonomic practices, instruments of knowledge and communication that are the conditions to form meaning and reach a consensus on meaning, do not exercise their *structuring* effectiveness unless they are also *structured* (Bourdieu, 1981).

With an education system where institutions and pedagogy do not seem permeable to that "inexhaustible epistemological difference of the world" (Santos & Meneses, 2009) that characterises vernacular cultures and non-formal knowledges emerging through participatory practices (an impermeability caused by subjection to the dominant normative standards), it is necessary to recover analytical perspectives that value useful epistemological alternatives to frame different ways of knowing. Highlighting and praising other ways of conceiving and exercising knowledge is ethically and politically significant because it deconstructs the techno-instrumental epistemic monopoly that strengthens the belief in knowledge that is free of worldviews full of limitations, presumptions and biases.

To put the monoculture institutionalised by educational systems back into perspective, it is therefore pertinent to emphasise vernacular experiences strictly linked to informal processes of transmitting and sharing *knowledge practices*, which would appear to refer to an archaic context, but which in reality they are always present in every corner of the world and are able to be revitalised and reshaped according to the contexts in which they take place and the instances of (re)signification (Baldi, 2011; Oliveira & Baldi, 2014).

So, unlike what modern science and government technocracy encourage, those forms of knowledge attentive to *situated* and *impure* knowledges are considered fertile ground, just as those respecting the countless ways of *making* and *conceiving* reality. They create space for alternative pedagogies and move away from standardised approaches, such as those inherited from the institution of *Homo educandus* and consolidated by the meritocratic ideology.

Continuing on the path of linguistic uses, the importance of valuing and studying the vernacular is again being discussed as an essential epistemological practice to understand and rescue communities – both peripheral and indigenous communities and subcultural communities of large global cities ("vernacular cosmopolitanism"). As pointed out by the philosopher Dismas Masolo in relation to indigenous philosophy and knowledges in African contexts:

> It is quite reasonable that each community has its own language, through which it expresses and conveys its values to its members. In fact, whoever engages in reflecting about the marvellous complexity of the language they call their own, or any others they know well, will quickly notice that its use is, in itself, a value, an art in which the performance of people is measured, admired and rewarded in several ways.
>
> (Masolo, 2009, p. 523)

Highlighting the postcolonial dimension of the changing relations between glocal knowledges and powers, Masolo emphasises the epistemological dimension of the vernacular as a powerful instrument of cultural difference and its dignity, but also as a lever to open it up to the syncretic fusion with other linguistic uses.

Although it seems quite obvious that the language of a community reflects the structure of its world, i.e. how it understands, defines and creates a taxonomy of its own ideas about itself, its relations, hierarchies and ecosystem, along with its values and dangers, only recently, with colonised peoples and cultures seeking liberation from colonial rule, has this reality received due attention (Masolo, 2009, p. 523).

In this sense, the groundbreaking lecture by the Brazilian scholar Paulo Freire (1979) is appropriately recalled. In it, Freire states that the goal of education is to help people (namely, those who were oppressed and marginalised) read their reality and write their own history, through the appropriation of linguistic and expressive tools that are closer to them and more easily available, so that they can become actors of knowledge, rather than its objects. The epistemological legacy derived from vernacular knowledges – namely, when these are interwoven with "knowledges based on defending and promoting the life and dignity of the oppressed" (Nunes, 2009, p. 227) – is one of the theoretical and practical aspects sustaining the "epistemology of the South" (Santos & Meneses, 2009). In fact, for the ethical and political purpose that comes with the analytical dimension of this epistemological approach:

> The assessment criterion for a given knowledge depends on the way it affects the condition of the oppressed. A pragmatic epistemology is, therefore, inseparable from recognising the constitutive character of normativity in the production and assessment of knowledge.
>
> (Nunes, 2009, p. 227)

In line with Illich's reflections, as well as the legacy of postcolonial anthropology and deconstructivist philosophy, based on the recognition of diverse forms of knowing (interpreting, sharing and producing knowledge), epistemological sensitivity through vernacular knowledges redefines the conditions in which each of those forms emerges, develops and is validated:

> The criteria that can determine the validity of those different knowledges stop referring to a single standard – scientific knowledge – and become inseparable from assessing the consequences of those different knowledges in their relationship with the situations in which they are produced, appropriated or mobilised.
>
> (Nunes, 2009, p. 233)

Current epistemological challenges make us value the *learned ignorances* ("docta ignorantia") that every experience and knowledge carry at their core: citing Nicholas of Cusa, Boaventura de Sousa Santos (2009) highlights how the diversity of human experience refers to "diverse knowledges about the human experience" (p. 466). Learned ignorance suited to our time would endow us with the (self-)awareness that "The less a given knowledge knows the limits of what it knows about other knowledges, the less it knows its own limits and possibilities" (p. 468). Vernacular knowledge, learned ignorance, the different cognitive and perceptive forms that guide indigenous cosmogonies, the practical reasons that sustain informal, collaborative and even scientific and institutional cultural practices all share the experience of the incompleteness, precariousness and partiality of their own world views.

However, as Pierre Bourdieu has incisively explained, learned ignorance should not be romanticised as if it were knowledge free from social conditioning and overdetermination. For the French sociologist, all knowledge has at its core an implicit and unconscious socio-political dimension that escapes its own reflexivity, guiding cognitive and perceptive principles based on the "divisions" of social structures that in turn mould "visions", practices and expectations about the same social world of reference.

Critical and anti-hegemonic epistemologies cannot avoid confronting the effects of what Bourdieu defined as "epistemic doxa", that silent evidence of doxa incorporated and reproduced by apparently spontaneous, free and self-conscious behaviour and knowledge. It is therefore important to prevent epistemology from reproducing doxology by analysing, for example, the historical evolution of knowledge and cultural practices rooted in different social contexts, the cross-relationships between expectations and aspirations, evaluating the conditions that provide the evaluation criteria themselves and critically comparing the consensus and conflicts latent in the "ways of life" that give rise to specific ways of thinking and feeling.

Promoting an epistemology open to "pluriversity" (Escobar, 2018) potentially makes scientific hierarchies and analytical categories more flexible, as well as challenging a respectful interest in the details of contexts and knowledge practices, where the explicit and implicit dimensions of understanding and valuing phenomena coexist and feed off each other. Moreover, as the Sri Lankan anthropologist Stanley Jeyaraja Tambiah (1990) has already pointed out, the evolutionist view that usually puts *magic*, *religion* and *science* in sequence is somewhat biased and mistaken, since far from representing opposing heuristic constellations, they actually represent coeval productions of human experience and thought that run in parallel and even overlap.

Going back to the technocratic impasse that subdues a large part of formal education systems, held hostage to competitive logics and their various ranking devices, we can re-examine the consequences of those logics in the fields of training and reconsider the possibility of other pedagogical processes inspired in "making the different world views and forms of knowledge symmetrical" (Nunes, 2009, p. 222), including those definitions of operational skills that become the object of situated assessment. If until now *Homo educandus* and meritocratic ideology reflected a system projected as the *cradle of the obedient*, the alternative epistemologies and reflexive pedagogy triggered a re-examination of the assessment of hierarchies between competencies, making way for pedagogical processes based on self-assessment. A strategy that would allow not to separate the learning context from its teaching practices and the behaviour of students, which would be useful if carried out under certain conditions, is a real autonomy of educational institutions, which decide how and what to assess, during which periods and with which purposes, previously ensuring a lived and shared knowledge of the material and cultural conditions of schools themselves and the social environment where they are located and with which they interact. This assessment would of course differ from school to school, since analysis of the context of departure could not avoid determining the quality and quantity of resources being used for the purpose: it would be a useful assessment to leverage transformative pedagogical strategies and challenge learning processes in favour of greater involvement and investment of other local resources, leaving aside the top-down ministerial rankings between good and bad schools (Pena-Vega, 2020).

Learning Through Shared Practices

However, as already mentioned, the epistemological gains of vernacular practices and sensibilities come from various (geo)cultural contexts and hemispheres. Rectifying the spatial metaphor mentioned earlier, both in the South and in the North of the world there are social dimensions that are both creative and hideous, both progressive and reactionary, both supportive and predatory. The margins, in their different guises, are ubiquitous and should not be ideologically typified or thought of as belonging exclusively to distant and distinct territories. Polarising and moralising knowledge processes and practices according to geopolitical metrics or socio-economic hierarchies means ignoring the jointly porous, coevolutionary, contrastive and transcultural dimension of socio-cultural processes, as well as feeding localist and manichean utopias.

There are many ethical and epistemic characteristics of the South that can be found in the North and many others of the North that can be found in the South. The historical and geopolitical processes of globalisation trigger cultural practices in constant disjunction, hybridisation, compensation, resistance, mimicry and differentiation, which are therefore capable of reverberating their conflicts and their ability to coexist at all latitudes (Appadurai, 1996). Fortunately, in fact, both in the pedagogical field and in the creative and productive field, it is worth noting how many schools, work contexts and Western cultural areas are innovating methods and logics of growth that are alternatives to utilitarian, productivist and rationalist monocultures (Escobar, 2018; Andrade & Ibarra, 2021; Tironi et al., 2023).

For example, returning to the field of design, whose economic distortion has conditioned many of its practices in the direction of marketing, ludification and programmed obsolescence, some critical and collaborative development projects are worth highlighting, focusing on social change through a reformulation of labour practices based on "far-reaching" processes (far-reaching present). Combining anthropological and design sensibilities, Mike Anusas and Rachel Harkness (2016) present in the chapter "Different presents in the making" (from the book *Design Anthropological Futures*) a harsh critique of a conception of designer work orientated by a temporality contracted into the "close-present". This tight conception of time is conceived as a linear sequence of tasks mobilised by the expectations of clients to increase their business, i.e. many creatives are part of a production system that calls on them to operationalise their knowledge in favour of a product capable of generating new profits for their clients. Daily experiences with compressed time (a child of presentist culture) reduce creative potential and sensitivities towards the environment, both labour and ecological. For the two researchers, who carried out field research in product design studios, the working environment conditioned by productivist objectives and tight deadlines leads to pressures, tensions and verbal expressions that reveal the irritation of not being able to manage time and the creative process itself, determining an individualistic and mechanised context (Anusas & Harkeness, 2016, p. 65). Even when we talk about ecological design, this is just another methodology applicable to product design, always subordinated to a temporal perspective compressed into a planned succession of close-present.

The epistemic and creative condition based on the *far-reaching present*, however, retraces the participatory design experiences that emerged in the 1970s in Scandinavia or those of community design inspired by Paulo Freire in different Latin American contexts (Andrade & Ibarra, 2021). These experiments aim to create an intersectional design ethic between the local and global, organic and inorganic, dimensions of tradition and contemporary becoming, promoting a "transitional design" (Escobar, 2018) that is productively autonomous from market circuits. For anthropologist Arturo Escobar, all communities based on sharing common interests (territorial as well as labour, artistic as well as political) practice design to the extent that they create the conditions for their members to participate in decision-making processes and in learning about these processes, creating their own ways of living and coexisting. By integrating these contexts, designers with an anthropological sensibility can speed up the creation of conditions for collaborative social change, supporting the individual and collective projects of the communities in which they work. The scenario of practices opened up by an attitude of *far-reaching present* promotes the design of solutions and innovations applied in communities and by communities, without following prescriptions and timescales dictated by outside interests, but rather endeavouring to create production systems that are closer and more sensitive to the ecosystem of reference.

The *far-reaching present* emancipates us from an intransitive and compulsory relationship with the present, as well as from an idea of a predictable, programmable future, hetero-determined by stubborn illusions of uninterrupted linear progression that, in reality, cage its potentialities and heteromorphies. The *far-reaching present* allows us to embrace a temporality punctuated by the relationship with what is inevitably contingent and exposed to the combinations of the different "interdependencies" that mould it.

With regard to innovative pedagogical projects for learning and assessment systems, those educational experiences that aim to provide learners with a subjective appropriation of knowledge methods, their representational languages and ways of producing and self-evaluating their own know-how deserve to be valued. Moreover, these educational projects promote training contexts where non-formal teaching-learning processes are provided, based on the in fieri appreciation of the competences that are acquired and discovered in progress.

As Henry Jenkins, Mizuko Ito and danah boyd recall in their book on *Participatory Culture in a Networked Era*, educators had believed for centuries that learning and cognition happen *in the head* of individuals and that education should be about getting information into those individuals' heads so they can carry knowledge around and apply it in different settings.

In spite of this established pedagogical perspective, since the last century the education system has witnessed, in various fields, people debate and forge a new paradigm for theorising and supporting learning in a participatory, non-formal manner. Researchers demonstrated through empirical study that learning is inseparable from the cultural identities, practices and material settings of everyday life. They argued that the education agenda should focus not on getting things into kids' heads but rather on supporting favourable contexts for students to develop a sense of belonging, participation and contribution to their own learning process.

Situated learning theory, in turn, not only aims to deconstruct the foundations of traditional (logocentric) cognitive theory, but also to challenge the core assumptions of our educational practice. Why should we be sitting kids down in rows to learn maths or philosophy in the abstract when it is both more engaging and effective to learn it in the real world or through meaningful social activity? Real-world and real-frame promote concrete comparisons in everyday problem-solving for a meaningful purpose (of learning).

Therefore, we can understand how important it is to emphasise the effectiveness of non-formal teaching methodologies in contexts that intend to develop complementary skills to those taught at traditional schools. Through one-to-one teaching and group facilitation, people all over the world have used non-formal education methods to pass on traditional knowledge and ensure that each new generation learns from the old.

A "culture of making" can be a good example of a non-formal approach to training and improving knowledge; it is, in fact, increasingly emerging as a focus of society at large. For example, there is a growing re-appreciation of practical skills in formal educational contexts, reflected in learning by doing approaches or the inclusion of arts and crafts schools at higher education level (Ingold, 2013).

We wonder whether these approaches point to a new appreciation of *bodily skills* and can be the first signs of doing away with the classic separation between body and mind in educational contexts.

The training experience based on the development of situational learning is seen as much more meaningful than mere skilled manual labour. The work process must do something that sounds distasteful to the tidy, clear mind, which is to dwell temporarily in messy or wrong moves, false starts, dead ends.

Indeed, in technology, as in art, the probing craftsman does more than encounter mess; he or she creates it as a means of understanding and shaping working procedures. At the same time, his or her experience is moulded by the transformative processes of disorder into new plastic configurations. *Making*, as also explored in the section on embodied cognitions, refers to an understanding that is both an absorption and apprehension of the elements that constitute learning processes, reflecting a practice inextricably entangled in an active involvement with the material and cultural world. Making is about understanding in practice and is inextricably tangled with an active engagement with the material world and culture. Still, it is important to realise that the notion of making has evolved in ways that differ from traditional craftsmanship.

We can also say that the making of culture is inherently participatory. Young people can be apprenticed to local blacksmiths, carpenters, seamstresses and tailors (but also journalists, designers, social workers, architects, doctors, etc.) to learn a trade through first-hand experience or on-the-job training.

However, the working philosophy of *makers* has attracted the interest of professionals, educators, practitioners and the academic community, in view of its informal, open, networked, peer-led and shared learning, its potential to create new pathways into knowledge development and its experimentation with new skills that allow us to understand and value the construction process more than the finished product.

Returning to Sennet, the sense of craft skills propels us towards perspectives of learning and commitment to the world that go beyond simple manual labour:

> "Craftsmanship" may suggest a way of life that waned with the advent of industrial society, but this is misleading. Craftsmanship names an enduring, basic human impulse, the desire to do a job well for its own sake. Craftsmanship cuts a far wider swath than skilled manual labor.
>
> (Sennet, 2009, p. 15)

Through pedagogical practices based on *situational making* in a non-formal tutoring context, we can also re-signify the clumsy relationship we have with digital technology. As we've seen before, platformised connective tools have acquired the characteristics of antisocial devices. Despite being received in educational contexts as gifts from the gods, because they can be an asset in the learning of various skills, these tools nevertheless "work against the learning of what are called 'social values', including the understanding of democratic processes" (Postman, 2002, p. 64). In this sense, as well as "training" learners in the use of new technologies, it is essential to immunise them against the risk of conceiving of problem-solving in isolation, of seeing the challenges of learning and growth in a separate, private and exclusive way.

Like all cults, that of technology also "aims to garner irrational loyalty and acquiescence" (ivi, p. 62), which is why it would be necessary to develop a critical awareness of its customisation from an early age and, conversely, to emphasise the value of those social skills of group life, of participation and trust that are consolidated in the experiences that are made with others, of linking the individual to those around them, learning directly to tame the "ego", in other words, to subordinate one's needs to the interests of the group. Personal recognition and individual self-realisation are truly emancipatory and healthy feelings when they derive from a social return based on the ethos of reciprocity, when they result from an ethical bond where *acknowledging* and *being acknowledged* play the same humanising role. When a technology becomes an instrument that fosters conviviality and working together, it regains its function as a means at the service of a purpose that transcends it.

In this sense, as shown by recent research on collaborative "knowledge building", learning processes grounded in collective inquiry, shared responsibility and epistemic agency challenge the meritocratic view of knowledge as individual performance and constant optimisation (Cacciamani & Khanlari, 2025). Such models align with non-meritocratic pedagogies that value slowness, dialogue, interpretive uncertainty and mutual recognition.

The philosophy behind a participatory education process is to encourage learners to express their learning desire and, not less important, challenge the group of trainees to represent and communicate the way they see the world and express something about their daily lives. To reach these goals, it is necessary to build up mutual trust and curiosity. *Making*, then, comes to fulfil its culturally emancipatory function when it acquires the characteristics of "worldmaking" (Goodman, 1987), that is, when it leverages a reconfiguration of the gaze, interfering and participating in a critical vision of society.

The emphasis on *metacognitive awareness* developed in collaborative learning research exposes the epistemic impoverishment produced by meritocratic environments. When educational systems reward speed, optimisation and outcome–centric assessment, they obstruct the reflective dimension required for meaningful cognition. For example, using the opportunities offered by new communication technologies, in particular when working with youth groups, different techniques can be used, such as: sessions with arts and crafts, drawing, theatre, reading and commenting on newspapers and websites, the creation of "photovoice" sessions through which they learn to use multimedia tools and languages to tell personal stories, playing sport and musical instruments or having informal conversations designed to generate interest sharing (Moura & Baldi, 2021).

The group facilitator works "in partnership and cooperation" with the youth, giving a "voice" and visibility to their reality, making them not only the "objects" of representation but the authors of it. Participatory culture is therefore conceived as a process that is constantly shaping itself by embracing the different values it has to deal with, a culture that assumes that we can make decisions, collectively and individually, and that we should have the ability to express ourselves through a wide range of languages and cultural practices.

The culture that is learnt and passed on by doing things with others makes it possible to express oneself artistically and become civically involved and can provide strong support for creating and sharing one's own creations, so that through some type of informal mentorship, what is known by the more experienced is passed on to the novices. A participatory culture is also one in which all participants, no matter what their role, believe their contributions matter and feel some degree of social connection with one another (at the least, they care what other people think about what they have created).

A non-meritocratic pedagogy, therefore, aims to restore "epistemic agency", understood as the capacity to pose questions, negotiate meanings and transform shared knowledge. This stands in sharp contrast to algorithmic-meritocratic models that reduce learners to data points within predictive and classificatory systems (Cacciamani & Khanlari, 2025).

Leaving the Meritocratic Ideology

Contemporary culture must bring to the centre of contemporary debates the type of citizenship it wishes to invest in. Paraphrasing Hannah Arendt, the type of *heritage intended for the future* must become a central part of the public discourse agenda; political communities that care about what *past to leave for the future* (Arendt, 1968) ought to be considered valuable. Through the German philosopher, we know that each individual can develop and realise their abilities to the extent that they value the common heritage received through their community, which they can continue if they are able to contribute in innovative ways. In this view, *heritage* and *heresy* coexist; there can be no political community without this double bond between a historical legacy and its vital transformation.

Returning to the critique of the illusory and instrumental conception of progress sustained throughout the book, it is once again relevant to highlight how this notion has been characterised as a *destiny*, thus stunting any other idea of the future and inhibiting the will to explore new paths in a heretical way. However, the notion of progress as a naturally emancipatory destiny was also questioned as ideologically *technocratic* by Walter Benjamin a century ago (Benjamin, 2003). Referring to Marx's *Critique of the Gotha Program*, Benjamin emphasised that the distinctive feature of technocracy is to equate social progress with technological progress and related capitalist accumulation.

The ideological scope of progress consists, in fact, of measuring quality of life based on the criterion of quantitative accumulation. However, this notion of progress is increasingly devoid of meaning, since its technocapitalist direction leaves behind even the guarantee of survival that once gave it meaning. If progress continues to be conceived through the prism of technological "salvation" and the concentration of wealth, knowledge and natural resources, then it will be difficult to change direction in favour of social progress, or rather, a future open to progress that is neither trapped nor opportunistically biased, but possibly enriching and meaningful for its inhabitants.

The education system is in a strategic position to be able to fulfil this challenge: to challenge the epistemological orthodoxy that it institutionally tends to reproduce and, linked to this, to confront the meritocratic logic that radicalises the economic culture, with its ethical consequences for individual, collective and ecological life.

If we decide that we are, first and foremost, citizens, then this means that each one of us – as Aristotle argued – is a *homo politicus*, in other words, a living being who is naturally social and concerned with justice, equality and ethics; if, however, we choose to embrace the "ecocidal" logic of *homo œconomicus* – this is the human subject according to the neoliberal paradigm – then we will always be in competition with each other, where the other is naturally seen as a competitor who will act in a regime of permanent rivalry. Common feeling (and thinking about the common) today seems to have been completely colonised by neoliberal paradigm. It is this impossibility of imagining a world that is not enslaved by economics that characterises our time; on the contrary, the "widespread economization of heretofore non-economic domains, activities, and subjects" (Brown, p. 31), such as health, education, respect for the environment, life itself, is accepted without challenge; after all, "we are everywhere *homines œconomici* and only *homines œconomici*" (Brown, p. 33).

However, meritocratic ideology, by disguising its violent reproduction of privilege, determines a psychological condition of constant guilt in those who don't fit the profile of *homo œconomicus*. Linking meritocratic systems to those of social ascension promotes cognitive and social injustices, since in the various spheres of society there are incomparable qualities and abilities, as well as structural inequalities in the conditions of access to the prerequisites for competing. By establishing a context of competition based on the cult of individual performance and the struggle of all against all, what we end up with is the opposite of merit, knowing that in the end it will be the "reason of force", and not the "force of reason", that will drive social ascension.

Meritocratic violence is sustained by a pseudo-logic that aims to hide and deny in an autotelic way the cynical, self-interested and arbitrary matrix that guides the conception of cultural capital (and the consequent training processes) that is presented as a model of civilisation. However, if we look closely, by sharing a condition of latent unease and fear in the face of the uncertainty generated by this pseudo-logic, we can assume our inculpability, since the responsibility for these malaises lies in the time of false certainties and false promises in which we are immersed. In this sense, rejecting the moralising blackmail reflected in the evaluative categories of "elected" or "winners" versus "losers" or "undeserving" allows us to relate and impute existential discomfort to that which is political and (in)civilisational. If what unites us is the sharing of stresses and concerns about our present and our future, then it becomes ethically and pragmatically necessary to call for other symbols, other directions and actions from which to establish new social and psychological priorities. The symbols of merit and success have in fact proved to be false and tainted by an antisocial ideology: "The individual's subjugation to the market is thus marked by delusions of autonomy and yet grounded in actual powerlessness" (Crary, 2022, p. 121).

Unlike those who appear to freely manage their destiny, here we have the pressing challenge of giving it a social purpose other than mere survival or movement for movement's sake, where "experience is reduced to what can be instantly searched online", despite knowing that "pathways to a different world will not be found by internet search engines" (Crary, 2022, p. 121). As we saw in the first part, there is an intrinsic relationship between ludification and illusion, just as there is an intimate relationship between media ecology, communication tools, interaction practices and cognitive and perceptual habitus. By participating in a culture traversed by *infopinions*, gamification, the adoption of stratagems to compete, the subordination of political institutions to the market and (among other things) the subordination of actions and beliefs to systems for predicting and anticipating virtual events, we have also damaged our ability to objectify and differentiate our own behaviour, leading to a relationship of strangeness in relation to our gestures and thoughts.

> In numerous ways, we are induced or compelled to follow the routines of digital work and leisure and to align ourselves with their mediocrity and mindlessness. [...] We convince ourselves that our goals and aspirations can be achieved through a dutiful and numbing conformity with the precepts and regulations of a system we know to be malign. We acquiesce out of passivity or convenience, and over time we come to have thoughts and gestures that are no longer our own.
>
> (Crary, p. 118)

Experience and the feeling of uncertainty can acquire an emancipatory potential if, first, they are not exchanged for incapacity, and if they are not moralised as guilt. The multitude that shares this experience can cross their existential impasse with the historical and ideological, transforming it into a political challenge, unleashing alternative ways of living and acting in everyday life, demanding and idealising new symbols and new designs that bring together projects based on rescuing differences, proximity, finitude and vulnerability.

Proximity, linked to the feeling of reciprocity, is the backdrop to a world that cannot exist if it is thought possible to separate the interdependencies between living species, the organic and inorganic worlds. The antisocial impulses of *homo œconomicus* must be countered with a concept of freedom that is immunised against the narcissistic presumption of being able to break the chains of interdependence that sustain us.

In this sense, training experiences become culturally promising when all subjects involved in them develop an allergy to the monocultures and standardisation of skills and goals. Training and the educational context, to quote Arendt once again, should become a testing ground for the "common world", in other words, that heterogeneous reality of beings, knowledge and interests in which we are all concretely involved. A common world understood as a stage for epistemic differences, which are always incomplete, partial, never self-sufficient and, therefore, challenged to coexist and co-evolve.

Notes

1 https://ec.europa.eu/programmes/erasmus-plus/anniversary_en.

2 Illich's first texts on education were published in 1971 in his book *Deschooling Society*, at a time when the social effects of mass schooling and compulsory education, triggered by a number of government institutions from the world's North and South, were starting to be felt. Since this publication, Illich has returned to the subject of education on very many occasions. His key purpose was not to attack schools or the potentially enriching opportunities resulting from teacher-pupil relationships, but rather to target the institutionalisation of teaching and pedagogical programmes, which he deemed to be the cradle of a new systemic process employing discrimination and guilt in relation to diverse experiences and diverse fields of knowledge.

References

Andrade, D., & Ibarra, M. C. (2021). Aproximações em Design para além do Racionalismo: tecendo caminhos para o pluriverso. *Estudos em Design*, *29*(1), 155–169. https://doi.org/10.35522/eed.v29i1.1155

Anusas, M., & Harkness, R. (2016). Different presents in the making. In Smith, R. C., et al. (Eds.), *Design anthropological futures*, 55–69. Routledge.

Appadurai, A. (1996). *Modernity at large: Cultural dimensions of globalization*. University of Minnesota Press.

Arendt, H. (1968). *Between past and future*. Viking Press.

Baldi, V. (2011). Os rituais são sempre contemporâneos: uma epistemologia do implícito. *Ateliê Geográfico*, *5*(1), 1–16. https://doi.org/10.5216/ag.v5i1.13722

Benjamin, W. (2003). *Selected writings*. Harward Univesity.

Bourdieu, P. (1981). *Le sens pratique*. Édition du Seuil.

Bourdieu, P. (1997). *Méditations pascaliennes*. Édition du Seuil.

Brown, W. (2015). *Undoing the demos: Neoliberalism's stealth revolution*. Zone Book.

Cacciamani, S., & Khanlari, A. (2025). Knowledge building in the artificial intelligence age: Exploring the role of large language models as students' consultant. *QWERTY*, *20*(2), 80–101. https://doi.org/10.30557/QW000102

Crary, J. (2022). *Scorched earth: Beyond the digital age to a post-capitalist world.* Verso.

Delors, J., (1995). *Enseigner et apprendre: Vers la société cognitive*. (European Commission report: https://europa.eu/documents/comm/white_papers/pdf/com95_590_fr.pdf)

Escobar, A. (2018). *Designs for the pluriverse: Radical interdependence, autonomy, and the making of worlds.* Duke University Press.

Goodman, N. (1987). *Ways of worldmaking*. The Harvester Press.

Freire, Paulo. 1979. *Educação e mudança*. Paz e Terra.

Illich, I. (1992). *In the mirros of the past. Lectures and addresses, 1978–1990*. Marion Boyars Publishers.

Illich, I. (2004). *La perte des sens*. Fayard.

Ingold, T. (2013). *Making: Anthropology, archaeology, art and architecture*. Routledge.

Latour, B. (1999). *Politiques de la nature*. La Découverte.

Masolo, D. A. (2009). Filosofía e conhecimento indígena: uma Perspetiva Africana. In Santos e Meneses (Eds.), *Epistemologias do sul*, 507–530. Edições Almedina.

Morin, E. (2003). *Éduquer pour l'ère planétaire, la pensée complexe comme méthode d'apprentissage dans l'erreur et l'incertitude humaine*. Balland.

Moura, I. S., & Baldi, V. (2021). Isto não é uma ilha, isto é um bairro: representações audiovisuais da comunidade do Bairro Herculano. *Discursos Fotográficos, 17*(30), 10–27. https://doi.org/10.5433/1984-7939.2021v17n30p10

Nunes, A. J. (2009). O resgate da epistemologia. In Santos e Meneses (Eds.), *Epistemologias do Sul*, 215–241. Edições Almedina.

OECD. (1997). *The definition and selection of key competencies. Executive summary.* https://www.oecd.org/pisa/35070367.pdf

Oliveira, L., & Baldi, V. (2014). *A Insustentável leveza da Web: retóricas, dissonâncias e práticas na Sociedade em Rede*. Edufaba.

Pena-Vega, A. (2020). *Les Sept Savoirs nécessaires à l'éducation au changement climatique – Comment les jeunes s'engagent pour l'urgence climatique*. Atlantique.

Postman, N. (2002). *O fim da educação. Redefinindo o valor da educação*. Relógio D'Água.

Sandel, M. J. (2020). *The tyranny of merit: What's become of the common good?* Penguin UK.

Santos, B. d. S., & Meneses, M. P. (2009). *Epistemologias do sul*. Edições Almedina.

Santos, B. de Sousa. (2009). *Um ocidente não-ocidentalista?: a filosofia à venda, a douta ignorância e a aposta de Pascal*. In Santos, Meneses (Eds.). "Epistemologias do Sul". Almedina, 445-486.

Santos, J. M., & Soares, A. (2022). The morality of numbers. *Electra, 15*. Fundação EDP, 7–12.

Sennet, R. (2009). *The craftsman*. Yale University Press.

Tambiah, S. J. (1990). *Magic, sience, religion, and the scope of rationality*. Harvard University.

Tironi, M., Chilet, M., Marín, C. U., & Hermansen, P. (Eds.). (2023). *Design for more-than-human futures: Towards post-anthropocentric worlding*. Taylor & Francis.

von Foerster, H. (1984). *Observing systems*. Intersystems Publications.

Wittgenstein, L. (1969). *On certainty*. Basil Blackwell.

Index

For Product Safety Concerns and Information please contact our EU representative GPSR@taylorandfrancis.com
Taylor & Francis Verlag GmbH, Kaufingerstraße 24, 80331 München, Germany

www.ingramcontent.com/pod-product-compliance
Ingram Content Group UK Ltd.
Pitfield, Milton Keynes, MK11 3LW, UK
UKHW022158190926
475702UK00003B/85

* 9 7 8 1 0 4 1 2 8 5 9 1 5 *